Spells for Peace of MIND

Spells for Peace of MIND

How to conjure calm and overcome stress, worry, and anxiety

Cerridwen Greenleaf

CICO BOOKS

LONDON NEW YORK

Dedicated to all of us who deal with anxiety, depression, chronic worry, fearfulness, and hypervigilance. And we are many! This book is intended to offer comfort, a helping hand, and practices that will bring you peace.

Published in 2019 by CICO Books
An imprint of Ryland Peters & Small Ltd

20–21 Jockey's Fields   341 E 116th St
London WC1R 4BW   New York, NY 10029

www.rylandpeters.com

10 9 8 7 6 5 4 3 2 1

A CIP catalog record for this book is available from the Library of Congress and the British Library.

ISBN: 978 1 78249 792 9

Printed in China

Editor: Marion Paull
Designer: Eliana Holder
Illustrator: Michael Hill
Photographer: Roy Palmer

Commissioning editor: Kristine Pidkameny
In-house editor: Dawn Bates
Art director: Sally Powell
Production manager: Gordana Simakovic
Publishing manager: Penny Craig
Publisher: Cindy Richards

Safety note: Please note that while the use of essential oils, herbs, incense, and particular practices refer to healing benefits, they are not intended to replace diagnosis of illness or ailments, or healing or medicine. Always consult your doctor or other health professional in the case of illness, pregnancy, and personal sensitivities and conditions. Neither the author not the publisher can be held responsible for any claim arising out of the general information, recipes, and practices provided in the book.

Contents

INTRODUCTION
Mind-Body Magic in the Age of Anxiety

When I reflect, I realize one of the greatest blessings of my life is growing up on the farm. I remember complaining as a teen about living "out in the sticks" but, thankfully, that was a brief phase. Daily walks in the woods kept me grounded, and growing herbs and wildcrafting in fields and meadows gave me a sense of purpose and taught me the importance of being self-sufficient. I also learned the very important lesson that we are here to help others and I'm glad that, in some small way, I am able to offer to lend a hand. That is how the book came to be.

Over the years, in large part thanks to my books, I have gathered a clientele. In the beginning, it was mainly love and prosperity spells, astrology and tarot readings, as well as designing rituals specific to my clients' needs. Of late, the most frequent requests have been around stress and anxiety. In the past two years, their needs have acquired a growing urgency. I live in the San Francisco Bay Area, home to some of the largest tech companies, such as Oracle, Tesla, Facebook, Twitter, and many more. Somehow this geek work culture has gotten very out of balance with people working 12- and even 15-hour days, which is clearly not healthy, nor is it sustainable—at all. The folks I help range from café baristas to teachers to managers at these big data firms. They all need help to regain balance in their lives. I am very happy to report many success stories, people who, through some of the spells and helpmates in this book, were able to deal with sleeplessness, constant worry, panic attacks, and disquiet. When you are trying some of the Office Magic rituals, know that some of the

gleaming glass towers in Silicon Valley have
crystal cairns and essential oil remedies
right there in workspace shrines in service
to stress relief and living in harmony.

I do love that the simple wisdom I brought
from my family farm can help people in the most
high-tech center of the world. I have discovered that
the homemade healing potions, teas, and cures our grandmothers cooked
up from the kitchen cabinet are the best things to turn to in tough times.
A veritable cornucopia of cures and pagan prescriptions for you to try are
to be found herein. In my own life I have dealt with anxiety and issues
around grief and loss in the past couple of years, so I can offer my own
testimonial to the supportive effects of these recipes, rituals, and spells.

It is my sincere hope that the suggestions here offer you and your loved
ones much relief from any stress and strain you might be experiencing.
Keeping your life in balance with nature is of the utmost importance.
A walk in the nearest park or even around the block during the work day
can be a mindfulness meditation. Mother Nature is the ultimate healer so
spending time outdoors in her abundant beauty will bring you much peace
of mind. Practicing the art of sacred self-care will enable you to thrive and
stay inspired so you can bring your special magic into the world.

Chapter 1

SACRED SELF-CARE
Pagan Prescriptions for a Whole, Healthy, and Happy You

To a great extent, the search for wellness and healing was the origin of witchcraft. While our forefathers tracked the sun and stars, looked for omens, navigated the wild, and learned the art of survival, our foremothers were figuring out which plants, roots, herbs, and flora were edible and, along the way, learned much about healing. The world was their laboratory and for today's witches, it still is. While we have come a long, long way from those early days of discovering which herbs were good to eat, drink in teas, and use in poultices to heal wounds and fevers, we are still learning the miraculous properties of plants for both physical and emotional healing.

Here is my strongest suggestion: you must create your own sanctuary, not just in your home but within yourself. You can have a safe space in your mind where you retreat to meditate, refocus, renew, and strengthen both your mind and spirit. I think of this as mental-health magic and it is of the utmost importance to integrate this sacred self-care into your daily life. Take good care of yourself. You are very much worth it and the better you are, the better our world will be.

goddess blessing: *a witchy wellness ritual*

Wherever you are along the pagan path, I have no doubt that you are being called upon to help your loved ones, your spiritual circle, and your community much more than ever before. The pressures of work, finances, constant connectedness, and the unrelenting barrage of negative news reduce immunity. Self-care is essential and, like many of you, I am drawing from everything I have learned from my wise Auntie Edie, my magical mentors, and all my experience and Book of Shadows recordings for what works well to counteract the dis-ease in our environment. In times like these, we are called upon to serve others. That is the intention behind this spell.

gather together:

1 green, 1 brown, and 1 blue candle

1 amethyst, 1 citrine, and 1 green jade crystal

sandalwood incense in a small fireproof bowl

a smooth flat stone, at least 10 in. (25 cm) in length

Tapping into the strength of earth is an important aspect of healing magic. This rite is best performed outdoors in the garden or on your fire escape or deck. Take the flat stone and designate it as your outdoor altar. Now, place the candles, crystals, and incense on the rock. Light the first candle, whichever color you prefer, and the incense and pray aloud:

The world is too much with us
But we have the power of our Mother Goddess.
The magic we bring to the world
Will help, will uplift, will serve, will heal.
Mother Goddess, I call upon you to make me a vessel
To help others in times of need. For this, I thank you.
So mote it be. Blessed be.

Light the next candle and repeat the spell. Light the last candle and say it again. Contemplate the candle flames as you draw strength from Mother Earth. You will know when it is time to put out the candles and incense. Store your mobile altar and, when you need to recharge, repeat the wish spell.

AL FRESCO THERAPY: *forest bathing*

According to a recent EPA (Environmental Protection Agency) study, the average person spends 87 percent of his/her life indoors and 6 percent more in a car or commuting in buses or trains. We don't spend much time outside. Stress has a major impact on health and aging—spending time in nature is a way to counteract that and has been shown to reduce anxiety and increase relaxation. Forest bathing, a practice begun in Japan in the 1980s, is growing in popularity and is blessedly easy. Forest bathers go to wooded areas and simply sit or stand in nature. Breathing in the air and taking in the earthy smells will bring your senses alive and, as a side benefit, regulate heart rate and blood pressure. Grab a camping blanket and set out to find a wooded area where you can be alone in the cathedral of nature. No phones! Find a spot, put down your blanket, take off your shoes. Stand on the forest floor barefoot and feel the earth under your feet. You can either sit or lay down on your blanket for at least an hour and just be.

Baking-soda basics

Baking soda (bicarbonate of soda) is great in a bath and is very calming to the skin. Add a cup (4½ oz/130 g) under the faucet (tap) as you fill your tub with hot water. If you suffer tension headaches, a simple solution is to treat it with a teaspoon of baking soda dissolved in a cup (8 fl oz/225 ml) of warm water with ¼ cup (2 fl oz/60 ml) of freshly squeezed lemon juice. Drink at room temperature and soon you'll feel fine.

POT OF GOLD: *aloe heals everything*

Even if you have the opposite of a green thumb, you can grow aloe—
and you should. We have an aloe plant in our kitchen. It is very sturdy—
I even left it out on the porch recently and can now attest that an aloe
houseplant can withstand freezing temperatures—and it's pretty hard
to overwater or underwater aloe. It's the perfect plant for beginners.
Any time a sting or burn needs soothing, pull a leaf and squeeze out
the gel onto the affected area.

I also have a huge plant out in the garden, which is great for
making batches of aloe gel. All you do is gather and wash the
leaves, peel the skin, and harvest the gel inside. You can store it
in the refrigerator for ten days. As a topical application, aloe-vera
gel is great for all kinds of burns, and it has been shown to have
therapeutic value in the healing of skin lesions caused by psoriasis.

We probably all know aloe as a summer necessity for relieving
sunburn, but with all of the nutrients it contains—it's full of
vitamins and minerals—it is no surprise that this super-plant offers
many physical and mental-health benefits as well. Aloe is one of the
few vegetarian sources of vitamin B12, and also contains vitamins
A, C, E, folic acid, and choline. Potassium, calcium, selenium, and
iron are among the 20 minerals it contains plus it has 19 amino
acids, eight of which are essential.

Stir two teaspoons of the gel into 1 cup (8 fl oz/225 ml) glass of
water for a refreshing aloe juice, which is a great general tonic
recommended as an aid to digestion, a stimulus for intestinal health,
and a gentle colon cleanse; or you could dilute the gel in an organic
juice if you prefer. Aloe can help to regulate appetite and sleep
rhythms thanks to the amino acid tryptophan, which aids in the
production of serotonin. Serotonin supports feelings of relaxation
and reduces depression. Recent studies indicate aloe's ability to
improve memory.

Taking aloe vera daily will do you the world of good, but even
just a couple of times a week will be beneficial. It can also be
imbibed neat and, if you don't have your own plant, the juice
is easily found at any grocery store nowadays, ready-made.

massage is medicinal:
mango feel-better butter bars

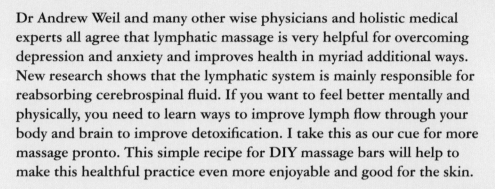

Dr Andrew Weil and many other wise physicians and holistic medical experts all agree that lymphatic massage is very helpful for overcoming depression and anxiety and improves health in myriad additional ways. New research shows that the lymphatic system is mainly responsible for reabsorbing cerebrospinal fluid. If you want to feel better mentally and physically, you need to learn ways to improve lymph flow through your body and brain to improve detoxification. I take this as our cue for more massage pronto. This simple recipe for DIY massage bars will help to make this healthful practice even more enjoyable and good for the skin.

gather together:

⅓ cup (3 oz/75 g) shea butter

3 oz (75 g) beeswax

1 teaspoon sandalwood essential oil

¼ cup (2 fl oz/60 ml) mango essential oil

double boiler

soap-bar molds (available at craft stores)

Slowly heat the shea butter and beeswax in a double boiler over low heat until just melted. Remove from the heat. Add the essential oils when the mixture has cooled slightly and stir. Pour into soap molds and leave to cool until hardened, approximately 2 hours. Place the molds in the freezer for a few minutes before popping the bars out of the molds. To use, rub a massage bar onto the skin—the warmth of the skin immediately melts the bar. I store some bars in small, travel-size tins so I have them available at all times.

THE HEALING POWER OF FLOWERS:
floral essence energies

Many of our favorite flowers have distinctive healing energies that can be captured in water. A key difference between flower essences and essential oils is that flower essences minister to the emotional body while essential oils treat the physical body. Vials of a multitude of flower essences are available at grocers, pharmacies, and new-age shops. Bach Flower Remedies are doubtless the most popular and have a recommended dosage of three to four drops taken via the bottle dropper under the tongue two to four times a day. I suggest using no more than two different floral waters at any given time for full effect.

Flower essences are typically ingested directly via the mouth or by way of adding a few drops to a glass of water. They can also be dropped onto linens, such as your pillowcase, or into your bath and can be applied directly to the pulse points (temples and wrists). Floral essences are also different from essential oils in that they do not carry the scent of the flower. It takes a few flowers to make an essence whereas essential oils rely on a significant amount of the plant.

bloom again: *sip a flower essence for a gentle remedy*

I am happy to share my family recipe, lovingly handed down through several generations. To make your own flower essences at home, start by making a mother tincture—the most concentrated form of the essence—which can then be used to make stock bottles. The stock bottles are used to make dosage bottles for the most diluted form of the essence, which is the one you actually take.

gather together:

handful of freshly picked flowers specific to the malady being treated (see Chapter 5)

6 pints (2.8 liters) fresh pure water or distilled water

organic brandy or vodka, at least 40 percent proof

large glass mixing bowl

tweezers or chopsticks

cheesecloth (muslin)

large pitcher (jug)

green or blue sealable glass bottles

Ideally, begin early in the morning, picking your chosen flowers (all of the same species) by 9 a.m. at the latest. This leaves you with three hours of sunlight before the noon hour, after which the sunlight is less effective, even draining.

Put the water in a large glass mixing bowl. To avoid touching the flowers, use tweezers or chopsticks to place them carefully on the surface of the water, until the surface is covered. Leave the bowl in the sun for three to four hours, or until the flowers begin to fade.

Now, delicately remove the flowers, being careful not to touch the water. Strain the flower essence water through cheesecloth (muslin) into a large pitcher (jug). Half-fill a green or blue 8-fl oz (225-ml) sealable glass bottle with the flower essence water, and top up with the brandy or vodka (this will extend the shelf life of your flower water to three months if stored in a cool, dark cupboard). This is your mother tincture. Label it with the date and the name of the flower. Use any remaining essence water to water the flowers you've been working with, and murmur a prayer of gratitude for their beauty and healing power.

To make a stock bottle from your mother tincture, fill a 1-fl oz (30-ml) dropper bottle three-quarters full of brandy, top up with spring water, then add three drops of the mother tincture. This will last at least three months and enable you to make lots of dosage bottles.

To make a dosage bottle for any flower essence, just add two or three drops from the stock bottle to another 1-fl oz (30-ml) dropper bottle one-quarter full of brandy and three-quarters full of distilled water. Any time you need some of this gentle medicine, place four drops from the dosage bottle under your tongue or add it to a glass of water. Take or sip four times a day, or as often as you feel the need. You can't overdose on flower remedies, but more frequent, rather than larger, doses are much more effective.

Essences that are good for emotions

* **Passion flower** connects us to our higher self and connects to the divine.

* **Lemon blossom** clears away mental fog, adds focus, and brings forth clarity.

* **Hibiscus** awakens chakra points and is good for sexual healing.

* **Nasturtium** creates a sense of roundedness and stops over-thinking and worry.

* **Grape hyacinth** releases past trauma and emotional wounds and reduces stress.

detoxing your relationships:
healthy relationships are good for you

A term we are hearing more and more of late is "toxic people," which is a kind of shorthand for friends, exes, associates who bring stress and disharmony into your life. A healthy decision would be for you gently to end the relationship in a cordial and clean way. Performing a ritual to acknowledge the end of a relationship is an important part of the healing process. This ceremony is intended to help you to resolve issues, tie up loose ends, and move on. It is very important psychologically, psychically, and emotionally to recognize the closure. This ritual is best done privately, although you may want the support of a carefully chosen friend. Many emotions are going to rise up and you can, gently and with love, put these feelings to rest and assign them a place in your life: the past.

To help you begin this new passage of life, think about and write down concerns, worries, and questions you may have about the relationships you are choosing to let go. If you keep these questions in a journal, you can reflect upon them later and on how your life has changed for the better as result of the detoxing ritual.

The questions may include:

* Do I wish to cut off all ties completely?

* If any kind of relationship continues with the individual, what are the safe and peaceful ways to remain connected?

* What are the aspects of the relationship I wish to be free of, such as fighting, dishonesty, and stress?

* What are the positive memories I want to keep?

* What fears do I have?

gather together:

a photo of you and the person, either together or two separate ones

an envelope

a pen

Go to a place in nature where you went together, for instance a lakeshore, a beach, a path in the woods, or a park. Take the photo(s) and place it (them) in an envelope. Write on the envelope:

On this date _____, I say goodbye to _____
(write in the date and the name of the person).

Say aloud:

Now I am free to pursue my happiness, a new love, and new people in my life. Good memories I will treasure and independence is my pleasure. I say goodbye to this part of my life and release all pain and sorrow.
I welcome the new and the good into my life.
I am clear.
I am free.
I am me.

Take the envelope and bury it where it will decompose undisturbed—no need to burn it or throw it in the water. Allow it to return to the elements, as is nature's way. There is no doubt that you will feel sad, and by all means, allow yourself to cry and mourn. Each tear releases toxins from your system. As you return to your home, you will feel lighter. Your conscience is clear and your future is bright!

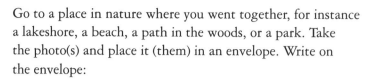

deep breathing: *for clarity, calm, and focus*

Your breathing is directly connected to your brain function and clarity of mind. The breath is controlled by your autonomic nervous system (ANS), which is affected by your thoughts. If you are feeling fearful or anxious about something, your thoughts will trigger the ANS to speed up the heart rate, raise blood pressure, and increase the speed and shallowness of the breath.

During every inhalation the heart rate increases slightly and during the exhale, the heart rate decreases slightly. This happens for everyone in every breath. As a result, you can wake up the body by taking a shorter inhale or de-stress by taking a longer exhale. Take a breath in for a count of three. Each number can be followed by a word—such as 1 Mississippi, 2 Mississippi, 3 Mississippi—to slow the counts to one second. Inhale for a count of three and then exhale for a count of six. You can also try inhaling for two and exhaling for four. As you lengthen your exhalation, instead of breathing out normally, try to hum as you do it. You might start off breathing shallowly but by the end of this practice you will be breathing diaphragmatically, from belly to nose. This is healing breath.

Deep breathing seems simple enough until you are experiencing stress and, without even knowing it, you'll begin breathing shallowly. Whenever that happens, try deep breathing as described above. Your stress will begin to fall away and your mental clarity will come into focus.

DIVINING A BRIGHTER FUTURE: *how to use a crystal ball*

Nothing is more vital than the breath, which is the source of all energy. It behoves everyone who uses a crystal ball to learn to control the breath. All professional seers, like all professional clairvoyants, cultivate deep breathing, for they are aware that their psychic powers are enhanced by their lung capacity. Deep breathing is a great aid to concentration, just as physical ease helps to erase irritability and ensure a patient attitude.

Three periods during the day are ideal times to consult the crystal ball: sunrise, midday, and sunset, although this does not preclude other hours between dawn and dusk. It is generally accepted that sunrise is the most propitious, for it symbolizes a new beginning. Times to avoid using the crystal ball are the dark hours from nine o'clock in the evening until dawn. During that period the scryer is renewing vital powers, either through sleep or meditation.

As a crystal-ball seer, you will notice clouding in your crystal, which may appear in various forms: as a milky obscurity, as a smoky, impenetrable mist, or as minuscule white clouds drifting through the crystal ball. White clouds are an affirmative indication of coming favors. If brilliance breaks through the clouds, it is indicative of the sun, which will light the way to better financial circumstances and to improved physical health. However, if a soft light lacking brilliance appears through the clouds, it is indicative of the moon, which foretells a period of inaction that may be likened to the recuperation of the vital forces.

* When the cloud is black, that is the time to be concerned, for a black cloud is unfavorable, even ill-omened. The seriousness of the prediction is measured by the degree of blackness. Does the blackness appear in a small portion of the crystal ball, or does it fill the entire globe?

* Occasionally, the clouds take on a show of color. If green, blue, or violet suffuse the crystal ball, this is an excellent indication. When green clouds appear, the individual will be called on to assist as a neighborhood mediator in an educational, political, or religious capacity. If a blue cloud appears, an occasion will arise that requires shrewd discernment and which will bring both honor and praise to the individual. When a violet cloud floats through the crystal ball, a latent talent may be recognized, or a worthy philosophical expression will be presented and well received.

* When clouds of red, orange, or yellow appear, the portents are ominous. Red clouds foretell dangerous situations—accidents, serious illness, and grief. Orange clouds predict loss of material goods and friendship. Yellow clouds bring deception and ultimate betrayal by supposed friends.

Chapter 2

COMFORT AND JOY
Creating a Harmonious Home Environment

I recently read a report saying that FOMO (fear of missing out) has been replaced by FOGO (fear of going out). While I am not sure that is altogether true, I do see a great return to nesting, cocooning together with loved ones to avoid the hard world outside. It is certainly no mystery why the Scandinavian concept of hygge (pronounced "hoo-guh") is on trend. There is no direct translation in English, but "cozy" comes close. Cozying up by a fire with books, blankets, and mugs of hot cocoa is delightful, but shutting out the world is not the final answer.

My sincere recommendation is to adopt an approach of fostering inner strength as well as buttressing your defenses with protective magic, so you can create a comfortable home base along with mastering the art of using energetic shields to protect against events and people who are psychic drains—all of which is covered in this book! Creating sanctuary is truly one of the most important things you can do for yourself and it will not only bring a long-term sense of security for you and your loved ones but also provide simple cozy joy and homey happiness every single day.

SUCCESSFUL SPELLWORK: *constructing your inner temple*

Call forth your powers within to make magic with ritual. Your mind and will are potent magical tools, and ritual is the practice of exercising your will. In order for your spellwork to be successful and a positive force in your life, you need to think a few things through.

First identify your intention, then plan and prepare for your ritual. Once you have gathered your essential ingredients and tools together, and everything is ready, you should relax completely before enacting the ritual. Afterward, clean and clear the space and leave everything in its place.

Setting your intention

A well-defined and focused intention is the key to success in a life-enhancing ritual. Good results depend upon clarity. If your intention is not crystal clear, you are likely to fail. You must approach your ritual concentrating fully on a definite aim. If a nagging worry is hovering in the back of your mind, you are not properly focused. You may even want to perfect an image of your intention and desire with creative visualization.

Part of your preparation should include using ritual correspondences— the phase of the moon, the day of the week, the color of the candles you use, and much more. These things add to the depth and meaning of your ritual. Do you need to clear the energy and refresh your altar with some housecleaning and smudging? Continue to focus on your intention while doing this; you are creating the foundation for a successful ceremony.

Mental-clutter-clearing visualization

While you are clearing energy in your space, you must also clear out the clutter in your mind. If you are in a state of inner chaos, the outcome will simply not measure up to your expectations. Perhaps it will help you to relax if you listen to instrumental music or sacred chants. Conscious breathing or stretching will also help you to prepare for the ritual.

Constructing your inner temple is a marvelous process that can aid your journey deep inside yourself. Sit or lie down in a position that is comfortable enough to relax you, but not so comfortable as to allow you to drift off to sleep. As you breathe slowly and rhythmically, imagine a place that you find peaceful and beautiful. It could be a white marble temple in a lovely sculpture garden under a still blue sky. It could be a mirror pool by a sacred grove. It must be pleasing to you, a place you can visit frequently in visualization. It can be any size or shape but should have certain aspects:

* **Center:** Your inner temple should have a single center from which you can access all areas of the temple. This center is a representation of your personal power center.

* **Reflective surface:** Here is where you can take a look at yourself spiritually. The reflective surface can be a scrying mirror, a crystal ball, or even a pool of water. You can use it to look at the past, present, and future.

* **Water:** Your inner temple can have any number of water sources, such as a waterfall, a well, a stream, or an ocean. Water represents our deepest levels of consciousness. Commune with your deepest self here.

* **Earth:** Here is where you ground yourself, and create manifestation. Take stock of your deepest desires and goals in a garden, forest, meadow, or wherever your imagination guides you.

Ideally, your inner temple has four doorways or gates, one for each of the four directions and elements. Once you have created your ideal inner temple, you can use it to perform rituals. You have created a permanent sacred space inside and outside this temple through visualization.

gather your guardians: *simple home shrine*

If something is making you feeling edgy or overwhelmed, there is an easy way to deal with it. Create a shrine at the source of your stress. If the problem is too heavy a workload, use your desk. If it is the onslaught of bad news from cable news, place it near the TV. My friends bent over laughing when they saw an army of goddesses in front of the TV recently but they also took notes as I explained how well it worked.

gather together:

1 statue of a deity of your choice, a god or goddess who can be your guardian

1 black and 1 white crystal—obsidian absorbs the negative; white quartz emits the positive

1 black votive candle and 1 white votive candle in glass votive containers; these small votives burn for 3 hours

sage for smudging and a fireproof dish

your broom

small bowl containing ½ cup (3½ oz/100 g) of salt

Set up your shrine by placing the ritual implements, including the statue of your chosen deity, on a table, shelf, or a flat surface in the relevant area. Put the black crystal by the black candle and the white one by the white candle.

Light both candles and use the black candle to light the sage. Go around the newly designated shrine, room, or area with the sage for a good smudging. Put the sage in the fireproof dish.

Now, take up your broom and with light strokes, sweep the shrine space thoroughly and brush the negative energy out of the front door.

Extinguish both the sage and the white candle and place them on your permanent altar. If you don't have one, place them in an area where you will see them regularly, such as on your nightstand. Let the black candle burn down safely in the glass votive container and discard the remains outside your home.

Get the bowl of salt and place the black crystal in it to cleanse the crystal of unwanted energies. Leave the white crystal by the guardian deity overnight.

When the new day arrives, thank the deity for protection and leave the statue and the white crystal on your permanent altar, nightstand, or wherever you prefer so you are reminded of protective and positive energy. Take the black crystal out of the salt and leave it on the shrine. Pour the salt onto your front step and sweep it away. Now, savor the serene feeling.

serene space spell: *a sweet and spicy brew*

Even if you don't subscribe to magic, you can probably guess that certain flowers and herbs have their own energies, in the same way as they have uniquely lovely scents and oils. Simmer a mixture of them whenever you feel the need to infuse your home and hearth with the energies of quietude and protection. This will safeguard you and your loved ones from outside influences that could be negative or disruptive.

gather together:

¼ cup (¼ oz/5 g) rose petals

⅓ cup (¼ oz/5 g) dried rosemary

1 tablespoon dried basil

¼ cup (¼ oz/5 g) dried sage

1 teaspoon juniper berries

1 tablespoon dried cloves

4 cinnamon sticks

1 medium-sized bowl

2 cups (16 fl oz/450 ml) water

1 medium-sized pan

1 wooden spoon

Put all the herbs, flowers, and spices into a bowl and gently blend the mixture together by hand. While you are doing this, close your eyes and visualize your home as a sacred place protected by a boundary of glowing white light. Imagine that the light runs through you to the herbs, flowers, and spices in your hand and charges them with the energy of safety, sanctity, and protection. In a pan, bring the water to a simmer and add the mixture to it. Stir with a wooden spoon. When the aromatic steam rises, intone:

Made of flowers and fire,
This brew brings the peace I desire.
With my hands, I make this brew
To bless our home and hearth anew.
And so it is.

I let the brew simmer for at least an hour. As the sweet and spicy fragrance imbues your home with cleansing energy, enjoy the blessings brought by this simple house magic.

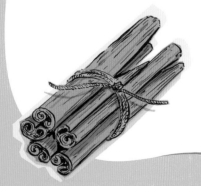

holy smoke: *hygge home-fire rite*

I heartily approve of the Danish tradition of hygge (see page 23) which is a lovely form of self-care togetherness. The Scandinavians integrate hearth fires into this custom so we'll take it one step further by adding sacred herbs on top of the wood for a cleansing, purifying, and therapeutic twist to hygge home fires. You can either bundle the herbs together with string or lay them on top of the unlit wood. I do both and speak this spell before lighting the fire in the fireplace. Alternatively, you could treat the barbecue like a firepit by removing the grill. Either watched by your loved ones or just by your lovely self, say the following:

Warmth and love, heart and heat,
Tonight, all good things we shall greet.
These sacred herbs will burn so sweet;
As we gather by this fire and merry meet.
And so it is.

Now light the fire and enjoy the holy smoke.

Sacred herbs for a fire rite

* **Mugwort** is an energy cleanser but also aids refreshing sleep and gives rise to meaningful dreams.

* **Cedar** has been relied upon for centuries to clear out negativity. The smell is very appealing and cedar is widely regarded as a sacred plant in varying cultures all over the world, where it is used to bless homes.

* **Sage**, beloved for smudging and space clearing, is greatly beneficial for meditation and a quiet mind.

* **Roses** bring sweetness and peace to any space and are also excellent for contemplation.

* **Sweetgrass**, highly prize by Native Americans, brings forth communal sense and a higher mind.

* **Bayberry** is considered lucky and brings pure, positive energies into your home.

* **Lavender** relieves insomnia, sadness, low moods, and anxiety, and brings comforting calm.

* **Juniper** was long used to produce purifying smoke in temples and is now believed to have revitalizing powers.

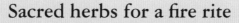

four-corners spirit spell: *add grace to your space*

You can purify your home every day, and in so doing, create sacred space.

Air purifiers you can grow

This is easy green magic, a great idea for both home and work. These plants don't take up much space and not only are they good to look at, they improve the air you breathe. Air-purifying plants produce oxygen, and can even absorb contaminants, such as formaldehyde and benzene, which are commonly given off from furniture and mattresses. These plants will purify the air in your home or office space 24/7:

* bamboo

* weeping fig

* rubber plant

* spider plant

* peace lily

* snake plant

gather together:

a bowl or cup (8 fl oz/225 ml) of freshly drawn water

½ cup (3½ oz/100 g) of salt

palo santo stick and a fireproof dish

Stand at the front door of your home and place the water, salt, and palo santo on a table near the door. Take the bowl or cup of water and add a sprinkle of salt. Then dip your fingers in the salt water and anoint your forehead with it.

Now turn to the east and speak aloud:

Spirits of the East,
You bring the rising sun.
I call upon you for new energy.
Purify this space and fill it with grace.

Now sprinkle droplets of water to the east. Turn to the south and say aloud:

Spirits of the South,
You bring us heat and rain.
I call upon you for new energy.
Purify this space and fill it with light.

Sprinkle droplets water to the south. Face west and say aloud:

Spirits of the West,
You bring us moon and stars.
I call upon you for new energy.
Purify this space and fill it with love.

Scatter some of the water to the west. Face north and say aloud:

Spirits of the North,
You bring us the air and winds.
I call upon you for new energy.
Purify this space and fill it with joy.

Scatter some of the water to the north.

Now light the palo santo stick and carry it with the bowl or cup of salt water to the four corners of your home. Sprinkle drops of water and let the purifying smoke of the palo santo waft around for a few moments. This same rite can be used in just one room, if necessary, somewhere there has been a quarrel, for example. In each corner, east, south, west, and north, thank the powers of that direction for their help:

Energies of the East [change for each corner],
I thank you for your eternal wisdom and sacred
support. We are grateful for your power divine.
Blessed be.

SPRAY YOUR TROUBLE AWAY:
DIY anti-anxiety home misters

Sometimes worry can be stealthy and surprise us with its arrival. Other times, it will make itself known loudly and clearly. What with the constancy of demands upon our time and energy, it is easy to understand why so many of us can feel anxiety. I urge you not to feel any shame about it. Ever. Many, many of us feel much the same way as you do and my intention with this book is to offer help so you can find what works for you.

The cause might well be a combination of a lot of little things. Take my own case as an example. People who know me well know that I love a strong cup of coffee, preferably a triple soy latte. I even thought of myself as a coffee achiever, running on pure caffeine, despite a lifelong love of tea. However, the routine of getting my beloved latte from my little neighborhood café went from a 10 or 15-minute event to over a half hour after a change of management and, worse, with uneven results. I started making coffee at home with even more unsatisfying outcomes.

So I began experimenting with herbal tea combinations and discovered my dream tea, which starts my day perfectly. It is a large cup of chamomile, cinnamon, and apple. The splendid scent, delicious taste, and heat is something I look forward to each morning. As if that is not enough, I noticed a side benefit. If I have it right, as I open email each day, I am undaunted by any digital onslaught that has come my way, and I realized that, even though I was just looking for my ideal morning beverage, this sturdy cup of tea was also reducing my anxiety. Find your little helpers and incorporate them into your sacred self-care.

happy home spray: *to refresh, restore, and uplift*

This blend smells wonderful, almost like you're walking through an orchard in full bloom. The aroma is fresh, fortifying, fruity, and floral. Neroli is excellent for calm and reducing anxiety, lemon refreshes and uplifts while tangerine sends sadness away, and quickly. Spritz this happy home spray in shared space, such as the living room, and in your bedroom for optimal rest and restoration. You can also very lightly spritz it on linens and towels.

gather together:

2-fl oz (60-ml) spray bottle (small blue glass ones are widely available)

2 fl oz (60 ml) distilled water

6 drops neroli essential oil

6 drops lemon essential oil

6 drops tangerine essential oil

Fill the bottle with the distilled water, leaving room at the top for the oils. Add in the essential oils and then seal the lid tightly. Shake vigorously and it's ready for use.

Rise with rose spritz

Follow the same simple steps and amounts as for the happy home spray but instead of the neroli and citrus oils, use rose, lavender, and bergamot to make a calming and comforting spray that will literally lift your spirits.

* Rose will give a sense of overall well-being and positively awaken the nervous system.

* Lavender helps deal with depression, unease, worry, and woe.

* Bergamot is an amazing mood booster and engenders optimism and hope.

For both of these self-healing spritzers, you can enhance the new energies with this chant:

Dearest goddess of us all, our Mother,
May this essence bring brightness like no other,
Nature's purest healing synergy
Will bring to us positive new energy.
Blessings to all. Blessed be me.

CULTIVATING CONTENTMENT:
your secret sorcerer's sanctuary

I tell people that gardening is my therapy and they always think I'm joking, but I am not. It is an enormous source of peace in my life. Pulling weeds and plant tending is a very positive way to handle nervous energy or upset. It also helps me to work out problems. After a wild and weedy session, I come back indoors feeling calm and in control. Combining the divine with the beauty of the plant kingdom can bring great pleasure to your life, and after the work is done, you can enjoy the fruits of your labors—literally if you have fruit trees and berry bushes.

A green thumb is hardly necessary to create your own secret sorcerer's plot. I am an advocate of garden statuary and, if you were to come over for a sip of tea and garden gazing with me, you will see an altar adorned with deities and a few carefully placed statues. What seems sacred and inspiring to you and is pleasurable to your eye will certainly do nicely. Even if you have a deck, a fire escape, or sunny windowsills, you can create your own sanctuary. Indoor gardening can absolutely fulfill the desire for an otherworldly aesthetic.

It will come as no surprise that, for a truly witchy garden, you should choose plants that love shade or look best in the moonlight. The rare art of magical gardening serves to put you in closer touch with nature, which is essential to pagan horticulture and is an amazingly peaceful pursuit. Working directly with the earth and her plants and flowers will teach you the secrets of our Great Gaia. Tending and growing these herbs and flowers will usher you into a very specialized world. From this vantage point, you can dry herbs to make special teas, potions, tinctures, and flower essences that are uniquely healing and magical.

Planting peace of mind

Grow these plants not just for their beauty and delightful scent but also to use in your spellwork, tinctures, and sacred self-care:

* lavender
* roses
* rosemary
* chamomile

* mint
* wooly thyme
* jasmine
* lemon balm

* passiflora
* sage
* geranium

new moon: *sowing the seeds of positive change*

Nature is the ultimate healer. The new moon is the time to plant seeds for the change you desire. If you want more calmness and less stress, sow the seeds for that. Go to the nursery or hardware store and buy seeds for a serenity garden: lavender, thyme, mint, chamomile.

You can do this at any time of year if you plant the seeds in herb pots on your windowsill. If the weather is warm and you have an outdoor space, plant them there and make that your outdoor serenity space.

After you have planted your herb seeds, pray aloud:

As these seeds grow,
More tranquility will flow.
Healing Mother Earth and Sister Moon,
I turn to you to bring calm and serenity soon,
Under this new moon and in this old earth.
So mote it be. Blessed be to all.

Gently water your new-moon garden, and affirmative change will begin that very day.

Chapter 3

OFFICE MAGIC
Warding Off Work Worries with Stress-Relieving Spells

We have all had myriad work experiences, from the first summer job at a café or shop through the first permanent job, possibly moving on to a larger company or a major corporation. No matter the size of the company, or whether you work from home as a freelancer or are revving up your own startup, it is never smooth sailing the whole time. Working life has a lot of ups and downs and you need to be able to roll with all of that. Work stress is an issue for most of us, so I encourage you to develop your workplace wellness routine.

If you can be strong within yourself, that will help you to weather any storm that comes your way, be it a demanding boss, grumpy coworkers, crazy deadlines, or complaining clients and customers. People compliment me on my shoulder-dusting crystal earrings, never realizing they are helping me to focus, stay sharp, and assume calm and equanimity. Whatever works for you, stick with it and make sure to practice workplace wellness and self-care in the form of work-life balance. It will be your saving grace and also the key to your success.

sunrise support ceremony: *welcome the new dawn*

Mornings set the tone for your day and this is the perfect time to ensure your day will be one filled with blessings and positivity.

gather together:

1 feather

1 yellow or gold pillar candle

bergamot essential oil in a stopper bottle

neroli essential oil in a stopper bottle

cinnamon incense

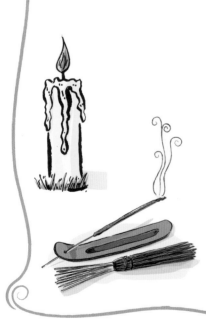

Take your bird feather and use it to carve symbols of happiness into the candle—hearts, clouds, sun, even words that, for you, represent joy and all good things, such as love, bliss, delight, glee, whatever gladdens your heart. Now anoint the candle with the essential oils, both of which are supremely elevating scents that will give a lift to your day. Light the candles and place them on a table where you can see the morning sun as it rises in the sky, spreading warmth and hope over all.

Light the incense and fan it with the feather, because birds are the harbingers of the new and messengers of change. As you breathe in the scented smoke, pray aloud:

I welcome the warmth of the sun inside of me,
I know my deepest wish is real and right.
I will my spirit to be free
Under this golden star in this bright, good light.
Spirits of peace—bless this space with all due grace.
So mote it be!

Take a few moments to feel the power of the sun and breathe in the invigorating scents of the incense and the bergamot and neroli. Repeat the chant one more time before extinguishing the candle and the incense. If this dawn ritual works well for you, as I suspect it will, you may want to incorporate it as a regular part of your routine, daily, weekly, or monthly. When something is helpful to your personal well-being, keep doing it.

lemon balm calm: *start your day rite*

If just looking at your to-do list and hearing the constant alarms from your digital calendar have you harried and at your wit's end, you need this lemon-balm herbal remedy. Lemon balm makes good on the offer the name implies—it is truly a balm for the soul. It can also soothe the heart and any lingering upset, and overcome blue moods and aches and pains from trauma, both physical and emotional. This tried-and-true potion creates a sense of inner calm that guarantees smooth sailing. But I do recommend that you change your calendar alarm to a nice chime that rings with the sound of serenity. Perform this rite either first thing in the morning or when you get to your work station so that you ease in to your day with a sense of peacefulness and purpose.

gather together:

8 drops carrier oil: jojoba or sesame

4 drops lemon-balm essential oil

2 drops chamomile oil

2 drops bergamot oil

small glass bowl and metal spoon

dark-colored storage bottle with a dropper lid

Drop all the oils into the bowl and stir gently with the metal spoon. Carefully pour into your bottle and seal the lid. Shake gently and next time you go to work or your office space, take it with you. Before you turn on your computer or even check your to-do list, give the bottle a gentle swirl and touch one drop onto your left inner wrist, associated with the heart. Rub your wrists together until the balm is on both of them. Lift your left wrist to your nose, close your eyes, and breathe in deeply.

As the serene scent awakens your senses, say aloud:

As I begin this blessed day
I know this tranquility will stay.
Nothing will get in my way.
And so it is; as I say.

Repeat the chant, and now you can begin what will surely be a blessed work day.

SIGILS: *choose your symbols well*

A simple and profound way to deepen your magic is to carve symbols on your candles. What symbols are meaningful to you? Certain crosses, vines, flowers, hieroglyphs, and many other images have deep magical associations, so you should feel free to delve into this and experiment to find the symbols that work best for you in your spells.

The term "sigil" is derived from the Latin *sigillum,* meaning a sign. A sigil is a magical glyph or symbol that is used in ritual to deepen focus or intensify magical powers. Methods for devising sigils include using the planetary glyphs of astrology, runes, Enochian tablets (which use wisdom from the Gold Dawn tradition of magic), letters, numbers, or even mystical ciphers, such as hermetic crosses or kabalistic signs. However, if you are like me and have limited artistic talents at best, you might choose to keep your sigils simple, such as a star, a peace sign, a cloud, a moon or sun, or a yin-yang symbol to represent balance.

The wisest choice would clearly be a visual symbol that you truly *love,* such as your favorite deity, an image of the sacred imbued with meaning. Even better, choose an image or symbol that expresses your spiritual belief. Although the word "sigil" generally means a seal or a signature, our magical sigil refers to a glyph used as a focus in ritual or sympathetic magic. The heart is a universal symbol of love, and a sweet design featuring a heart would make an excellent blessing to a romantic relationship or gift to loved ones.

Sigil magic

Any time you make or obtain a new candle for your altar space or personal shrine area, I recommend you take a moment to carve a meaningful symbol into it. Here are some options:

* Triangles arranged with the base at the top represent the Christian Holy Trinity as well as Egyptian spirituality and wisdom.

* Your astrological sun sign glyph, and that of your moon sign, is a lovely personal stamp.

* Double triangles signify all of creation, the conjunction of male and female and infinity.

* A hexagram is a symbol of the heart chakra and, in Hinduism, it indicates Kali in union with Shiva. If you want to create a mandala for blessing a relationship or to open your heart, the hexagram is an excellent choice. Combining the heart symbol and hexagram would signify a powerful love intention.

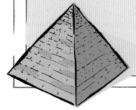

fire of focus: *inspire abundance and success*

The world is very distracting so paying extra attention to keeping our focus goes a long way toward creating a successful working environment. Create a small shrine at home dedicated to abundance at work. It can be your home desk, a shelf, or wherever works for you.

gather together:

citrine or any yellow crystal or stone

1 yellow candle and 1 orange candle

benzoin incense

incense burner or fireproof dish

neroli essential oil or orange-blossom essence

bergamot essential oil

sage leaf

Arrange your shrine in a way that pleases you and stimulates your senses. Place the citrine crystal beside the yellow candle and put the benzoin—a herb for all-around mental strength and clarity—in your incense burner or fireproof dish; it will bring inspiration from the psychic realm.

Now, using the dropper in the bottle of essential oil, anoint the orange candle with the neroli oil or orange-blossom essence; then anoint the yellow candle with bergamot essential oil while you meditate to clear your mind of any distractions. This is an essential step in opening the mental and spiritual space necessary to create, whether your intention is to create a ritual of your own design or to work on an art project or an Excel spreadsheet.

Once you feel focused, light a sage leaf and wave it around gently so the cleansing smoke permeates your shrine space. Light the anointed candles and the incense and wait a moment as the scent wafts around your newly dedicated space. Now set and speak your intention aloud:

With heart, soul, and mind,
And by the blessing of the spirits,
The fire of my focus
Burns steady and strong.
My mind is clear and sharp.
I bring my intentions into being.
The fire of my focus
Burns eternal.
Blessings to me and all who enter this space.

Let the candles and incense burn for 30 minutes before extinguishing them. Clean the incense dish and keep the candles for future rituals. Your work shrine will serve you well.

working wellness: *grounding spell*

One of my good friends is a psychologist who specializes in helping people with issues around work. According to Dr Helen, the number-one issue that causes panic attacks, anxiety, insomnia, and extreme stress is pressure from work and, oftentimes, overwork. I see this among my own circle of friends, especially those who work in tech and in Silicon Valley. The old wisdom of witchcraft can be very helpful for this thoroughly modern malady. Take matters into your own hands, literally.

Go into your backyard, a nearby meadow, or woodland and look for some loose soil. Pick up a palmful of the soil, hold it in your hands, and say aloud:

Mother of us all, I ask of you
To bring an end to what makes me blue.
No overgiving and overwork will I do.
From now on, I will stand strong and true.
Blessings to all.
Blessed be me.

Now rub the soil between your hands and meditate on feelings of peacefulness and stillness. Gently sprinkle it back to Mother Earth. Look around for small stones and take a few that appeal to your eye. When you get home, wash them and let them dry. Take at least one of the pebbles to work and place it on your desk where you see it often. It is your reminder to have healthy work habits and also to stay grounded. If worrying thoughts race into your mind, send them right back out by taking the stone into your hand and going back to the memory of when you did the grounding spell. Remember how the earth felt in your hands and how peaceful you felt. Breathe easy.

CHALICE OF CHOICE: *symbol of the feminine*

Your chalice is a goblet dedicated specifically for use on your altar. My beautiful office-magic chalice is made from Mexican recycled glass and I love the bubbles and irregularities that make it feel good in my hand. The various colors in the glass meld together for a somewhat post-modern stained-glass effect. I treasure my planet-positive chalice and, from it, drink healthy smoothies, spring water, herbal iced tea, and all manner of energy-boosting libations that everyone needs while working.

In terms of a wiccan implement, the chalice is a vessel that, like the cauldron, symbolizes the feminine, the Goddess, female fertility, and our ocean-covered Mother Earth. Holding both fluid and the waters of our emotional body, it is elementally connected to water. Place your special chalice on the left side of your work shrine with all other representations of the energy of the female and the Goddess.

A chalice is also a grail. After all, King Arthur's legend recounts that the Holy Grail brought life back to the decaying kingdom at Camelot and restored Arthur and his people, giving rise to the rebirth of England itself. On your permanent work shrine, your goblet can hold water, mead, wine, juice, or anything you wish to partake of or deem appropriate as an offering to share with the deities.

work well: *energy-boosting spell*

Here is a simple spell to observe a sacred healing moment during your working day. All you need is your favorite drink in your chalice of choice. Hold the filled glass and say:

As I drink this healthful cup
I ask the goddess to fill me up
With energy, inspiration, and joy
And in all my work, this I will employ.
So mote it be.

Magic in the office

Those of us who do not work from home can create a sacred work space in the office with a chalice. For your office shrine, and especially if you work in a busy office where a lot of witchy implements would raise too many eyebrows, you can keep it simple and choose a glass or cup that you really like to be your chalice. Take a moment each day to speak the chant and drink from your chalice.

Beryl, the efficiency stone

Beryl has a most unusual and important healing asset—it prevents people from doing the unnecessary. Furthermore, it helps the wearers to focus and to remove distractions, and therefore become calmer and more positive. Beryl also strengthens the liver, kidneys, and intestines, as well as the pulmonary and circulatory systems. It is especially effective for the throat and is invaluable for those who have to talk a lot in their work. Some crystal healers use beryl along with lapis lazuli as a sedative for nervous conditions. If you get overwhelmed at work or have a huge task ahead of you, efficiency-enhancing beryl will get you through it.

office tools: *ritual of consecration*

What do you use in your line of work? Select one item to represent your purpose and profession. I write and a pencil represents my occupation perfectly. If you are an artist, perhaps a brush would be a good choice, or a calculator for an accountant. Now that you have selected your special tool, you need to bless and dedicate it to your magical workings. This is an opportunity to fill your working day with more of your personal energy; you are encoding it with your unique imprimatur. Of course, use your excellent common sense here and don't sprinkle water on any electronic devices or dip any tool that will be ruined by salt. In these cases, you can pass the tool over the water and salt.

gather together:

1 cinnamon stick incense for air

1 white votive candle for fire

1 cup (8 fl oz/225 ml) of water

bowl of salt

Light the incense and the candle. Take your chosen ritual tool, and pass it through the incense smoke, saying:

Now inspired with the breath of air

Then pass the tool swiftly above the flame of the candle and say:

Burnished by fire

Sprinkle the tool with the water and say:

Purified by water

Dip the tool into the bowl of salt and say:

Empowered by the earth

Hold up the tool with both hands and imagine an enveloping, warm white light purifying the tool, and say:

Steeped in spirit and bright with light

Place the now cleansed and energized tool on your altar and say:

By craft made and by craft charged and changed. This tool [here fill in the actual name of the item] *God and Goddess, I hereby consecrate this tool.*

Accessories for success at work

It is no accident that kings, queens, and emperors wore crowns. The ancients expected their leaders to be wise, and a bejeweled crown bestowed the brilliance and power of the gems on the crowned person. While you may not want to wear a tiara to the office or a crown to the grocery store, you can wear hair clips and barrettes (hairslides) with crystals and stones attached for some of the same reasons. Why not be smarter and smartly accessorized? Bejeweled barrettes worn at the temples confer wit and wisdom, a kind of brain-boosting power energy. Here are some stones to choose from:

Tiger's eye can help you filter out mental distractions; excellent for research.

Turquoise is a good stone to help keep your mind and thoughts clear.

Fluorite is a true crystal of the mind and is very good for escalating mental focus. This blue crystal helps with multitasking and managing a great deal of information.

Sodalite brings clarity and insights and combines logic and intuition—a great combo!

AFFIRMATIONS WORK:
encouragement leads to accomplishment

I learned this about 15 years ago when I was recovering from a road accident, a hit-and-run by a drunk driver who had no insurance. My right arm and leg were broken in multiple places and I couldn't go to work or even walk. I opted not to take any pain medication (stoicism runs in the family!) and there were many rough and painful days, stretching into weeks. I did get to read a lot, which was wonderful. Those of you who have weathered broken arms know how hard it is to wash and comb your hair, let alone style it! So I was not at my best.

A dear friend, who brought me loads of magazines and books to read, sensed I needed a pick-me-up and gave me a Louise Hay affirmations card deck, a sheaf of colored paper squares, and a set of colored pens, and assigned me to write my own affirmations, once I'd learned how to do it from Louise. At first, I felt silly saying the affirmations from the deck aloud since I was feeling very blue. After a few days, I saw the value and, taking my friend's advice, began creating my own affirmations, which looked like those of a kindergartener, since my writing arm and wrist were in a cast.

For me, my most-used affirmations are the ones I crafted on the back of napkins at my favorite coffee shop once I was able to crutch my way over there. I forgot my DIY affirmations from my friend's sweet gift and borrowed a pencil from the handsome barista and set about affirming myself. Maybe it was the strong coffee or maybe it was the beauty of the day, but I still have those affirmations and use them to this day.

positive incantations: *compose your own*

As you will discover, when you write your own affirmations, a few of them will "stick" and really hit the spot. Here is what you need.

gather together:

paper cut into squares, ideally 12 squares

your favorite pen

1 votive candle

Go to your favorite spot for writing and lay out the paper, pen, and candle. As you light the candle, speak aloud:

I am strong beyond measure
I am loved beyond measure
I deserve a life of joy and pleasure
And so it is!

Breathe in and out deeply three times and sit down to pen your affirmations. Here are some suggestions to start you on your path:

* "I am a wholly unique person and I celebrate that."

* "I am open to positive change in my life and welcome it."

* "Every day, I am healing and growing in wisdom."

Write at least three. Keep them on your office shrine or altar where you can see them every day.

abalone ebullience spell: *thursdays bring opportunity*

Gorgeously iridescent, abalone shell is another of Mother Nature's healers, engendering feelings of peacefulness, self-compassion, and love. The gentle energy is warming and so soothing to the nerves, calming inner turmoil. Abalone can take you from worried to ebullient. Thursdays are named for Jupiter, or Jove—originally Thor of Norse mythology— who represents joviality, expansion, and all things abundant. Here is a Jupiterian Thursday spell that will bring excellent business and work opportunities your way.

gather the following:

1 abalone shell

1 purple votive candle

1 green votive candle

purple flowers of your choice

When you go to work one Thursday, take an abalone seashell, a bunch of flowers, and two votive candles—one green and one purple. Place the candles inside the abalone shell. Encircle the shell with the flowers. Stand in front of your natural altar and consider the wonderful, full life you are going to enjoy. Light the candles and say:

As above, so below,
The wisdom of the world shall freely flow.
To perfect possibility, I surrender.
So mote it be.

Extinguish the candles and keep for future usage. I am fortunate that a coworker gifted me battery-operated candles that can be turned on and off at the flick of a switch. They are perfect for work stations where candle burning would be frowned upon. They do wonderfully in a pinch and offer a twinkly light you might love.

Flourish with fluorite

Any fluorite reduces electromagnetic pollutants and cleanses the aura. Get a big chunk of fluorite at your favorite metaphysical five-and-dime/pound store and put it right beside your computer to decrease stress. Those long hours of staring at the screen will cease to sap your energy. Look at your fluorite at least once an hour to reduce eye and brain strain, too!

Violet—or amethyst—colored fluorite is especially good for the bones, including the marrow. This crystal opens the third eye and, best of all, imparts good old common sense!

Green fluorite is favored for its ability to ground and center excessive physical and mental energy.

Clear fluorite awakens the crown chakra and helps you to let go of anything preventing spiritual development.

Blue fluorite facilitates mental clarity, orderly thought, and the ability to be a master communicator.

Yellow fluorite kindles the synapses and awakens memory. It will also make you smarter and boosts your creativity.

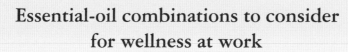

Essential-oil combinations to consider for wellness at work

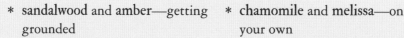

* sandalwood and amber—getting grounded

* ylang ylang and grapefruit—no worries

* clary sage and mint—sanctuary

* chamomile and melissa—on your own

* rose and geranium—life is sweet

* bergamot and neroli—high spirits

career candle magic: *color craft*

Candle magic is a mainstay of office magic. I burn candles every day and take them with me when I am traveling. For this exercise, simply apply the basic precepts of color magic: set your intention clearly on the outcome you desire and choose the appropriate color candle from the list below. Light the candle on your altar or in any special place in your home on the day mentioned, and let it burn for at least 5 minutes. Repeat this ritual on that day for seven consecutive weeks, using the same color candle.

* **Gold** is great around work, for influencing your boss, a promotion, fame, or success. Burn on Sundays.

* **Silver** can be used for your work space or home, subconscious, or emotions. Use on Mondays.

* **Yellow** is best for disputes, ambitions, goals, and confidence. Highest power on Tuesdays.

* **Green** is good for improved communication, research, data, and intelligence. Try Wednesdays.

* **Blue** is brilliant for legal issues, funds, spirit, security, integrity. Best on Thursdays.

* **Purple** is the power color for aesthetics, design, relationships, the arts. Burn on Fridays.

* **Black** helps with obstacles, judgment, decisions, property, protection. Use on Saturdays.

zen sensation: *pulse-point potion*

No matter what work you do, there will be moments when you need to take a short break to regroup and refresh yourself. This comforting and calming potion will do just that. Keep this homemade helpmate in your desk drawer where you can access it any time you need it. The subtle combination of almond, coconut, lavender, and vanilla is deeply comforting and uplifting. In a mere 10 minutes, you can whip up a spa retreat in lotion form. This is so quick and easy, you will doubtless add preparing it to your list of calming crafts.

gather together:

½ cup (4 fl oz/125 ml) almond carrier oil

⅓ cup (2½ fl oz/75 ml) coconut oil

¼ cup (2 oz/60 g) shea butter

2 tablespoons beeswax

1 teaspoon each of lavender essential oil and vanilla essential oil

sealable tin or heat-proof glass jar; 4-fl oz (125-ml) closed containers are easy to pop in your bag and take to work

double boiler with water

wooden spoon

labels and pens

Combine the almond and coconut oils, shea butter and beeswax and heat gently in the double boiler. As the water heats, the ingredients will start to melt. Stir intermittently with your wooden spoon to blend. Once the mixture is melted, turn off the heat and remove from the stove. Once it has cooled for 5 minutes, gently fold in the essential oils so the batch is thoroughly infused. Pour into your storage containers, seal, and label.

The lavender essential oil brings deeply tranquil feelings and vanilla is very comforting so this combination is ideal for a sense of zen positivity. In addition to using the lotion on your hands, put a tiny bit on your fingertips and apply to your pulse points, such as your temples, wrists, over your heart, and at the base of your throat. Close your eyes and breathe in the delightful and relaxing scent and reclaim your zen.

Chapter 4

SERENITY STONES
Crystals for Calm and Healing

We have a vast healing and life-enhancing trove of beautiful and sacred stones from which to choose, and each stone has its own inherent, divine qualities. Each one is unique for the energy it emits and how it interacts with our subtle energy field, or aura. In the same way that no two fingerprints or snowflakes are alike, each crystal is completely individual, never to be repeated again in nature.

Crystals found in nature are imbued with special qualities from the minerals and rocks surrounding them. Geologists are fond of explaining the varying colors of crystals as chemical impurities. I prefer to liken the development of crystalline color to the making of a fine wine, whereby the soil and even the neighboring trees, plants, sun, and rain affect the grapes and the resulting nectar. Gems, too, have notes, like a perfume or a wine or even music.

The use of gems and crystals in rituals, spells, and affirmations has been part of the human experience for millennia. By incorporating this practice into your life, you will create a flow of positive energy that will enable you to enhance your work, your family, your love, and every other part of your existence.

TOUCHSTONES FOR PEACE OF MIND: *crystal cairns*

A small stack of rocks, known as a cairn, may look purely decorative but it is much more than that. It is an important device to help you be in balance with nature. Many of our modern maladies, such as anxiety, SAD (seasonal affected disorder), tension headaches, depression, and more come about as a result of disconnection from nature. These stones serve not only as visual reminders of being in balance, but also have healing properties that surround you with supporting energies from earth. Crystal cairns are literally grounding for you. I am sure you will come to find this to be true. Certain crystals can be true touchstones in your life and bring multitudinous benefits, both emotional and spiritual.

Find a spot in your home or office where you can incorporate your crystals into each and every day, whether a shrine, your nightstand, or a corner of your desk. This can be your special corner of the world where you can renew and connect with your spiritual center. As well as simply looking at your cairn, picking up and holding your touchstones can be one of the most soul-nourishing small acts of self-care you can do.

Different crystals bring different benefits. Select which stones to include in your cairn according to your needs. As an example, a dear friend of mine was having extreme difficulties with a housemate. She started sleeping poorly and was on edge all the time. I stopped by with some chamomile tea to help her rest at night and three stones for her nightstand: pink quartz to help her reopen to love for herself and others, a Herkimer diamond for serenity, and a bright yellow citrine to tap into positive energy. She was skeptical at first, but reported back a few days later that simply gazing at her crystal cairn put her at ease and helped her overcome her interpersonal issues. When she asked for a crystal cairn for her housemate, I knew the crystal curative was a success.

Revitalize with rose

If you want to jump-start your life and bring about positive change, tap into the power of the rose and red stones. Stones on this side of the color spectrum contain life's energy and can help you become more motivated, more energetic, and more vibrant, and also give you an appealing aura. Wear these rosy and red stones or place them on your desk and throughout your home for an instant boost:

* alexandrite

* carnelian

* garnet

* red coral

* red jasper

* rhyolite

* rose jasper

* ruby

Crystal benefits

* **Inspiration:** Amazonite, aventurine, carnelian, chrysolite, chrysoprase, citrine, green tourmaline, malachite, yellow fluorite

* **Intuition:** amethyst, azurite, celestite, lapis lazuli, moonstone, selenite, smoky quartz, sodalite, star sapphire, yellow calcite

* **Love:** amethyst, magnetite, rhodochrosite, rose quartz, twinned rock crystals

* **Abundance:** bloodstone, carnelian, citrine, dendritic agate, diamond, garnet, hawk's-eye, moss agate, peridot, ruby, tiger's-eye, topaz, yellow sapphire

* **Protection:** amber, apache tear, chalcedony, citrine, green calcite, jade, jet, smoky quartz

* **Self-belief:** azurite, chalcedony, chrysocolla, green tourmaline, rutilated quartz, tiger's-eye

* **Serenity:** amber, aventurine, blue jade, dioptase, Herkimer diamond, jasper, kunzite, moonstone, onyx, peridot, quartz, rhodonite

* **Confidence:** carnelian, obsidian, quartz, selenite, sodalite, topaz

* **Positive energy:** agate, aventurine, bloodstone, calcite, chalcedony, citrine, dioptase, emerald, garnet, orange calcite, ruby, topaz

* **Deep wisdom:** emerald, fluorite, Herkimer diamond, moldavite, serpentine, yellow calcite

EARTH STONES: *moss agate for mental grounding*

Moss agate, which is quartz that has a plantlike pattern caused by metallic crystalline grains, is a power stone associated with the metal-rich planet Mercury and all things related to the mind. The ancients actually thought the dark green markings inside the stone were fossilized moss. They used moss agate for water divining, so it was especially sacred to farmers. It makes a great grounding stone for anyone who can get too caught up in their thoughts, and is a wonderful crystal for those who need help in keeping their feet on the ground. If you ever find your mind racing or worried thoughts creeping in, get your hands on a moss agate and you'll feel the reassurance of this rock.

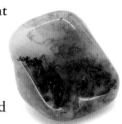

rock steady: *a grounding ritual*

Simplicity is the key to the effectiveness of this rite. All you need is a candle and a rock.

gather the following:

1 brown candle

1 moss agate or other earth stone (see facing page)

Take the candle and crystal and place them both on the floor. Light the candle and sit in front of it with your stone in your hand. Touch your stone to your forehead and say aloud:

Worry and fear
Are no longer here.
This is my touchstone, strong and true,
Come what may, I have the power to renew.
With harm to none and blessings to all,
So mote it be.

Now close your eyes and hold the stone in both your hands. Notice how a feeling of grounding rises up through your body to the top of your head. I keep my moss agate on my work shrine and if times are especially intense or worrisome, I carry it with me, just as it is or in a little bag.

Earth stones for centering

* Jasper: This stone has been valued for its healing and grounding energies since ancient times. Jasper stones carry very strong earth energy, helping to deepen your personal connection with the earth when you wear or meditate with them. I recommend either brown or red jasper, both of which are healing stones that also give you great strength, heighten energy, and have a lovely reinvigorating effect on your body.

* Smoky quartz: Smoky quartz is another beautifully grounding and stabilizing crystal that brings powerful energies for centering the body. This particular quartz has the effect of making you feel deeply rooted to the earth. It is very centering in an uplifting way, having a much subtler energy than hematite. Smoky quartz works to counteract any negative vibrations, replacing them with the positive.

* K2: This crystal has recently become more popular, but it will be a new discovery and a revelation for many people. K2 is a combination of grounding *granite* and celestial *azurite*, which balances our earthbound life experiences with our higher consciousness and connection to the universe and the heavens. It is an extremely powerful way to connect to your intuition and find the balance between your intuition and your daily life. If you are wrestling with a real issue in your life or need to make a difficult choice where the options are unclear to you, call upon K2 and use it in meditation. Soon, the answers will come.

* Shungite: Here is the most powerful stone for balancing. Shungite will inspire you to deal with your emotions, toxic thoughts, and anything that no longer serves you. While it can be unpleasant to look at these personal issues, it is a healthy thing to do. What you gain from this exercise is the grace and strength to cut the energetic cords that hold you back from your personal power.

witch craft: *amethyst circle-of-protection ring*

A few years ago, a major renaissance in crafting began, starting with knitting, crocheting, and beading. All our grandmothers and great aunts already knew the enormous benefits of such handiwork hobbies but when college students and people of every age started forming knitting circles, it was a remarkable sign. Fun scarves, sweaters, and hats may have been the end product, but crafters widely reported these hobbies to be therapeutic and a real aid to anxiety. Indeed, these handicraft projects and pursuits are very calming. Every moment you wear this sweet bead ring, you will be guided, guarded, and protected. Every gesture you make will be supernatural when you wear your circle-of-protection ring!

gather together:

44 tiny amethyst beads, easily available at any craft or bead store

18 in. (45 cm) of thin elastic thread (this will accommodate differing finger sizes)

2 sewing or wire-thread needles; make sure they will go through the holes in the beads

Multipurpose jewelry glue

Begin by blessing the beads on your altar or workspace:

This gift of the earth so fair,
Stone of serenity, gem so rare,
I call forth all guardians of the air,
Bless these beads and hear my prayer.
Fill each crystal with love and care.
So mote it be.

Next, thread the needles onto each end of the elastic thread and then use one of them to string four beads to the center of the elastic. Thread the left needle through the last bead on the right-hand side. Pull it tight, forming a diamond shape. Next, string one bead on the left thread end and two beads on the right. Thread the left needle through the last bead on the right. Pull it tight. Repeat until all the beads are used. In order to close the ring, thread the left needle through the end bead of the first diamond, instead of the last bead on the right. Pull tight, tie the ring off with a double knot, and place a drop of glue on the knot. Once the glue has dried completely, put on your ring. Notice how everyone is looking as you sparkle by!

Calming crystal beads

Once you get the knack of this project, you can try it again and vary the number and type of crystal beads. You can also wear more than one for a "stack of serenity."

 * Lapis lazuli for a keen mind

 * Red coral for a sense of inner strength

 * Turquoise for tranquility and grounding

 * Opal will give you intuition

 * Moonstone for higher self-esteem

 * Citrine for ease in communicating

 * Lace agate for feelings of confidence at work

 * Rose quartz for love of self and others

SELF-ESTEEM STONE: *rose quartz*

We all get worn down now and again and, when that happens, we often feel blue or at least in the doldrums a bit. If you have no other crystal, make sure to have rose quartz on hand. It infuses you with self-love and brightens the vibe anywhere it is. I view self-love as a superpower and the real foundation of all true personal power. Widely known as the stone of unconditional love, the soft pink hunk of love known as rose quartz is said to attract and inspire love in all forms. It's especially good for promoting self-love and emotional harmony. It can be a teeny tiny pebble of pink or a big ol' rock but you should have it near you, especially when you are feeling low. I say have some around at all times but, then again, I have crystals in every room. Keeping a piece of rose quartz out where we can see it, on your desk at work, on your nightstand, or next to the bathtub, can act as a powerful visual reminder to take a little bit of time for yourself.

sacred stone power: *find healing, balance, and ease*

I don't know about you, but many of my friends, family, coworkers, and I are experiencing extremely high stress. Therefore, I feel called to offer what small wisdom I have about what you can do to counteract this lack of balance in your environment and our world. As you will have realized having read thus far, I am a strong believer in the calming and healing power of crystals. People ask me, "How the heck could a piece of rock help heal my body?" I point to the wisdom of the chakra system. Sacred stones directly affect the etheric or energetic body.

It is becoming widely known that crystals can be curative for the emotional body, the spiritual body, and the physical body, and we have learned that crystals can interact electromagnetically with people. Prehistoric medicine men and shamans knew instinctively how to harness this stone power and use it to enhance or stimulate energy; they never doubted the power of the unseen. Modern shamans talk about the body in a different way; they are in tune with, and work with, the etheric body, the subtle life force that sustains the physical body and serves as the matrix for the metabolic functions. They work with the chakras (points of energy in the astral body that are associated with various parts of the physical body) and endeavor to make sure everything is in proper alignment. Illness beginning with misalignment of either the etheric body or physical body can result in a domino effect of maladies. Imbalance in the etheric body can cause low energy, depression, stress-related diseases, and any number of other serious physical issues.

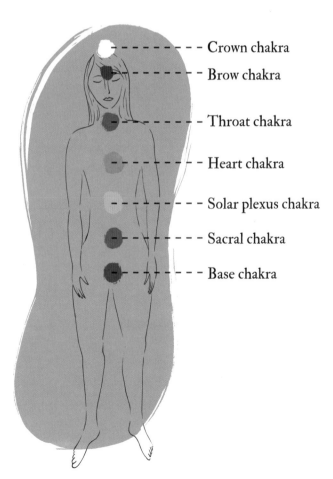

- - - - - - - Crown chakra

- - - - - - Brow chakra

- - - Throat chakra

- - Heart chakra

- - - - Solar plexus chakra

- - - - Sacral chakra

- - - Base chakra

Stress-reducing stones for you to try

Alexandrite will bring lots of zest. Feeling depressed, worried, and blue? **Citrine** or jet can banish dark days. Stressed out? **Rhyolite** races to the rescue.

Certain green stones, such as **chrysocolla** and **malachite**, calm the mind, and green-flecked bloodstone is a stress buffer.

If you want to be uplifted, try **jade**. To become wiser, pick **sapphire**. To stay safe while traveling, pick **dendritic agate**.

To remain calm and overcome stress, choose **blue lace agate**. For more mental clarity, choose **malachite**. For a self-esteem boost, try **rhodonite**.

Herkimer diamonds are power stones, bringing great vitality and exuberance into your life. They can redirect stress away from you with their absorptive abilities. Placing these rocks in your bedroom will cause the stress to melt away and help you relax and feel safe.

Dioptase is a gorgeous gemstone that is nearly the color of emerald but lacks the hardness, thus lowering its marketplace value. It can be found in Peru, Chile, Russia, Iran, and some sites in Africa. The true value of dioptase lies in its ability to help anyone experiencing mental stress. It lends balance to male and female energies and acts as a stabilizer. As an energy stone, dioptase can activate and awaken every chakra, invigorating the mind, body, and spirit. If you want to be really different, wear dioptase, and you will fascinate admirers with this beautiful stone and find peace of mind in the process.

supporting stone spell: *free what troubles*

Take your stone of choice and hold it in your hand while you speak this spell:

The world is heavy with woe,
I pray to let this burden go.
God and Goddess, I ask of thee
For less worry for our world and me.
So mote it be.

STONE OF SELF-BELIEF: *hematite vanquishes anxiety*

Hematite shores up self-image and self-belief. It also transforms negative energy into positive. Hematite is considered to be yang, a more male energy. My preferred aspect of this shiny wonder is that it assists with both legal problems and astral projection. Hematite is a creativity crystal and a marvelous mental enhancer, increasing the ability to think with logic, to focus, to concentrate, and to remember more clearly and completely. Hematite draws anxiety out of the body and creates calm.

In addition to all of these outward-projecting aspects, hematite contributes to inner work: self-knowledge, deeper consciousness, and wisdom. Like the iron in the earth from which it is formed, hematite grounds. If you feel spacey or disconnected, you should wear hematite. Hematite contains tremendous grounding energy that makes you feel like you are literally one with the earth. Touch it to your skin and feel the magnetic energy. It is this effect that will make you feel more balanced, calm, and centered. Hematite stones also soak up any negative energy within your body or energy field. After you have used it, you should place the stone in a bowl of pure salt to cleanse it.

Amber's emotional healing power

In Norse mythology, amber comes from the goddess Freya's tears that fell into the sea when she wandered the earth weeping and looking for her husband, Odin. Those tears that fell on dry land turned into golden amber. Now amber is believed to be very helpful and comforting to those who are separated and/or getting divorced, especially women, and to anyone who is experiencing grief.

DIVINATION STONE: *moonstone runes*

Moonstone is reputed to be the most powerful crystal for use in rune stones, the tools used for a specialized form of divination. Runes, or letters from a language used by early Nordic peoples, are carved into the stones and are said to hone and intensify the intuition of the reader divining the future from them. You, too, can use a bag of lustrous and mysterious small moonstones to get in touch with your powers of perception. While others throw the I Ching or read their horoscopes with their morning coffee, you can take out a moonstone, look at the pattern carved in its beautifully reflective surface, and contemplate its meaning for your day.

Scrying stones

The great seers can use a mirror, a still surface of water, or any reflective surface for prophetic purpose. Any polished stone can serve the same purpose. Here are some marvelous crystals for divination. Sit in a darkened room, hold the smooth stone in your hand, and gaze at it. It may take a few moments but you will begin to see flickering and even images on the surface. What you see are messages specifically for you. I suggest you keep a scrying record in your Book of Shadows.

* **Amethyst** opens your psychic abilities.

* **Azurite** with **malachite** can help you to conceive new ideas.

* **Bloodstone** guards you against deceit from others.

* **Celestite** gives you the very special help of angel-powered insight and advice.

* **Chrysocolla** helps you to foresee difficulties, including romantic ones.

* **Lapis lazuli** leads the way for the new in your life.

* **Selenite** can be used under moonlight for visions of your ideal future.

gratitude gems and lovely lodestones:
gifts from nature

Stones, crystals, and gems are regarded as the purest forms of the earth's generosity. Whenever you get a new crystal or a piece of jewelry with a stone or gem or decorate your home or garden with rocks and pebbles, show gratitude for these gifts from nature. This spell combines the power of crystals and that of thankfulness, which has been proven scientifically to improve mental health by Dr Robert Emmons in a study at University of California (see resources).

gather together:

⅓ cup (¼ oz/5 g) thyme

½ cup (¼ oz/5 g) daisies

⅓ cup (1 oz/30 g) ground cinnamon

1 stick of cinnamon incense

Sprinkle the daisy blossoms, thyme, and ground cinnamon on your garden path and on your doorstep. Push the incense stick into the ground by the path and light it. Stand on the threshold of your door and chant aloud:

Mother Nature, I thank you for the strength
And bounty of your stones and bones.
Your beauty is reflected now and forever.
Blessed be all, Blessed be thee.

Leave the flowers, herbs, and spice on the path—every time you step on them, you are activating blessings. Your gratitude will be rewarded tenfold, and you will enjoy a shower of crystals and gems in your life from Mother Nature, who enjoys getting credit for her good works!

heart-healing gem: *jade rainbow ritual*

If you are hurting, choose jade of the color that suits your need best (see below) and say:

My heart is heavy and hurting,
I ask the universe for relief.
Harm to none but release for me,
I long to heal and be free,
And so it is.

Colors of jade

* **Purple jade** heals a broken heart, allowing understanding and acceptance in and pain and anger out. If you are going through a breakup, purple jade will help you with the heartache.

* **Green jade** is the counselor stone and can help a relationship that isn't working to become functional instead of dysfunctional. This shade is also a boon for the brain. Green jade helps with getting along.

* **Red jade** promotes the proper release of anger and also generates sexual passion. Serve your lover a passion potion in a cup of carved red jade while wearing only red jade. Sparks will fly!

* **Blue jade** is a rock for patience and composure and for conveying a sense of control. Wear blue jade pendants for serenity.

* **Yellow jade** is for energy, simple joy, and maintaining a sense of being a part of a greater whole. A yellow jade bracelet or ring will help you to feel that all is well in your world.

LEPIDOLITE: *let go of your worries stone*

Lepidolite should be called the letting-go stone. It's like a fresh breeze coming into a room filled with stale air. In elixir form, it's a wonderful way to deal with addictive behavior or to ride yourself of old patterns that no longer serve you or are potentially unhealthy. This uncommon mica, an ore of lithium, has only recently come onto the gem and mineral market. It is shiny and plate-like in appearance, usually occurring in a pretty, pearly pink or purple color. On occasion, it appears white, and very rarely, it shows up in gray or yellow. This mineral occurs in Brazil, Russia, California, and a few spots throughout Africa. My favorite specimens are the single, large sheets of the lovely mica, which are called books and are an unforgettable violet.

Lepidolite is a great stone for getting a handle on anger issues. It soothes unresolved resentments, hatred, and frustrations. It is another mental stone and amplifies thoughts. Lepidolite is almost like a fairy stone in that it attracts positive energy, brightens spirits, and increases intuition. This is one powerful chakra healer, particularly for the heart and base chakras. One of the most important uses for this stone, albeit with great care, is for healing issues resulting from incest. Lepidolite is so powerful that you can even help manic depression and schizophrenia with it. When I had a bout of upsetting dreams and nightmares—unusual, as I usually have pleasant Piscean dreams—lepidolite came to my aid.

If you are lucky enough to come across a lepidolite that has fused with a rubellite tourmaline, then you have a rare rock indeed, and one that has double the power of any other lepidolite. This mauve mica is a commanding tuner for the etheric body, raising the frequency, tone, and pitch of energy in your head. Chakra healers have reported that lepidolite sends energy in a gentle and profoundly medicinal way from the heart chakra to the crown chakra and back again, strengthening the "cord" attaching the etheric body to our body and soul, and to the here and now.

emotional detox rite: *release with lepidolite*

gather together:

6 small lepidolite stones

1 pink candle

One quick way to deal with negative and hard emotions is to place six small lepidolite stones in a circle and light a pink candle in the center of the circle. Hold one of the lepidolite stones in your left hand, for heart connection, and concentrate on what is holding you back, both spiritually and psychologically. With each issue, feeling, or concern, say aloud:

I let go of ___

Do this a total of six times for each issue, holding a different crystal each time and placing the stone back in the circle after speaking. Picture the problem going into the stone in your left hand. When you are feeling full of calm energy, usually after about 10 minutes, extinguish the candle and place the stones outside your house (where no one will pick them up) and know that you have rid your home, personal space, and psyche of these woes! Whenever you feel the need, let go with lepidolite!

Chapter 5

ESSENTIAL OIL ENCHANTMENTS
Aromatherapy, Floral Remedies, Baths, and Balms

Are you stressed out, feeling unwell, or do you simply have a case of the blues? Essential oils can help in so many ways and are wonderful for boosting your immunity and your mood! Turn to these scentful helpmates to help you deal with anxiety, respiratory ailments, headaches, and so much more. Sure, they smell good and even feel good on your skin but how do they really work to ameliorate depression and anxiety, improve skin conditions, alleviate problems with lungs and heart rate, and address so many other issues?

A German study conducted by Ruhr University found that "essential oils may affect a number of biological factors, including heart rate, stress levels, blood pressure, breathing, and immune function." Essential oils are unique in that they can be both a stimulant and soothing for us humans. The same oil can cause a different response based on application because these oils are adaptogens; they truly adapt to your individual needs. If you are feeling down in the dumps, for example, bergamot can be a major pick-me-up and one I have depended on for years. My clients and I have come to depend on the power of these natural healers for dealing with stress, anxiety, worry, and woe.

STRESS-BUSTING ESSENTIAL OILS:
how to use them

Put simply, essential oils have aromatic, fragrant molecules that can actually pass right through the blood/brain barrier, having a direct effect on the areas of our brain in charge of controlling feelings of stress and anxiety, and even panic and depression. For long-lasting benefits, it's a good idea to use a diffuser.

* Breathe in deeply, rub one or two drops in your cupped palms. Take a long, deep breath and apply to your skin—temples, wrists, or anywhere, for full body relaxation.

* As a quick pick-me-up, put a few drops on a handkerchief, cotton pad, or scarf and inhale as needed. You'll get instant calming support throughout your day.

* As a shower infusion, immerse yourself in essential-oil steam by adding a couple of drops in your shower. Remember to plug or cover the drain and inhale deeply.

Help-yourself cupboard cures

Just one of these marvelous medicinals will change your outlook on the day. Try two and you will have a new outlook on life. Experiment with different twosomes until you have found the best for you.

* **Marjoram** lessens fear, loneliness, and grief

* **Lime** is a spirit lifter

* **Jasmine** shifts moods upward

* **Roman chamomile** quells anxiety and soothes moods

* **Grapefruit** inculcates a feeling of happiness

* **Sandalwood** alleviates dark moods and lifts emotions

* **Basil** is effective against depression, worry, and fatigue

* **Clary sage** helps with insomnia, apprehension, and bad dreams

* **Frankincense** helps to calm breathing and nerves

* **Peppermint** reduces stress and tension

* **Geranium** is a natural sedative and releases negativity, stress, and depression

* **Neroli** is invigorating and helps to deal with anger, panic, irritation, or fear

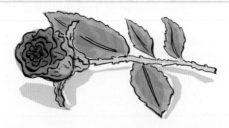

Aromatherapy for anxiety

Welcome the scent of serenity into your daily life with these essential oils.

* **Rose** essential oil is extracted from the flowers' petals and has an exquisite perfume. Rose is highly prized for how it relaxes you and also stimulates the senses and memory.

* **Lavender** is one of the most beloved of all aromatherapy oils and not just for the singular scent. It has been proven to relieve tension by the reaction of the limbic system in the brain that controls our emotions.

* **Jasmine** essential oil has an arresting floral scent, which can encourage an increased sense of well-being. Jasmine calms the nervous system without causing sleepiness.

* **Vetiver** oil is derived from the vetiver plant, a grassy native of India. It has a sweet, earthy scent and is used to attain a meditative state. It is a marvelous anti-anxiety remedy.

* **Basil** essential oil comes from the same herb that you use in cooking. In aromatherapy, it's used to help calm the mind and alleviate stress.

* **Clary sage** is a woody essential oil, valued for its anti-depressant qualities. It has been proven to reduce the body's production of cortisol, known as the "stress hormone."

* **Bergamot**, which comes from bergamot oranges, has a revitalizing citrusy scent. It is beloved for the way it can uplift and improve mood.

* **Ylang ylang**, extracted from the flower of the tropical cananga tree, is highly floral and a great relaxant, also proven in scientific tests to lower tension, reduce blood pressure and even heart rate.

* **Chamomile** is pretty well-known for its relaxing and sedating properties and its appealing scent. Chamomile can help to overcome sleep disruptions and bring about a good, deep rest.

* **Frankincense** oil, which is made from a tree resin, is cherished for its sweetly musky aroma, used to create a meditative state and ease anxiety.

* **Lemon balm** has a bracing and uplifting scent, which is very soothing and restorative and can also be a sleep aid.

* **Valerian** has been used since ancient times to promote sleep and calm nerves. It can have a mild sedative effect on the body.

* **Patchouli** has a musky, woodsy scent and is used in ayurvedic medicine to relieve anxiety, stress, and depression.

LAVENDER ESSENTIAL OIL:
the best-loved adaptogen

Lavender is beloved for good reason—it is one of the best and most commonly used adaptogens because it appears to adapt to any mood. An instant refresher, the sweetly serene and floral aroma is relaxing and calming. Applied topically, lavender oil is excellent for mental concentration, reducing stress tension, calming upset, and alleviating insomnia.

From the breath to your brain

Put two or three drops of lavender oil in your palms, rub rapidly, and, nose in palms, take a deep inhalation. This way the smell enters the amygdala, the brain's center for emotions, and provides a feeling of instant relaxation. If you have skin sensitivity, put the drops on a clean, dry, cotton cloth, such as a handkerchief. I advise keeping some lavender oil at your work desk and also carrying a small bottle when traveling. Heck, keep some with you at all times!

Headaches, begone!

Dab a drop of lavender oil on your temples near your hairline when you have a tension headache and it will begin to diminish right away. If you are looking for even more relief and relaxation, put some on your pulse points, such as your wrist, and on the soles of your feet.

lemon and lavender lift blend: *to soothe and soften*

This is a miracle mix of oils that you should massage into your body for both stress relief and a moisturizer.

gather together:

4 drops lavender oil

2 drops lemon oil

4 drops clary sage

5 teaspoons of your favorite carrier oil, such as sesame

small, dark dropper bottle

Put all the ingredients in a small, dark-colored dropper bottle and shake to mix. Keep this blend handy!

orange and spice: *for massage and much more*

This can be used as massage oil gently applied to pulse points. As a bonus, it repels bugs and can be great to use on a hiking or camping trip.

gather together:

4 teaspoons apricot or jojoba carrier oil

4 drops cinnamon leaf essential oil

6 drops orange (neroli) essential oil

small, dark dropper bottle

Pour these oils into a small, dark-colored dropper bottle. Shake gently and store in a dark cupboard for when you or your loved ones need perking up.

Gently massaging the pressure points on your body human body is both pleasant and very therapeutic. This practice relieves pain, increases circulation, and perks up your personal energy. There are many pressure points to be found in soft tissue near bundles of nerves and joints. All should be kneaded tenderly. For optimal healing, speak these soothing words:

As my energy flows, so does my healing grow.
Pain and stress do not serve me.
Peace of mind, body and soul, come to me now.
Harm to none, healing to all. So mote it be.

Cinnamon leaf: an instant boost

Cinnamon leaf oil is delightfully spicy with very effective anti-inflammatory properties. It works wonders for relieving aching muscles and all aches and pains after a long, hard day. Cinnamon leaf oil is a true boon for reducing stress and anxiety. I put a few drops of it in my diffuser because it instantly relaxes me. The tension just drains away and I feel more content.

It also helps to reduce drowsiness and will give you an instant energy boost, perking you up when you're feeling exhausted, both physically and mentally. Put one or two drops on your wrists or on a clean hankie or cotton swab and inhale directly.

The spicy aroma is sure to revitalize you!

START WITH SELF-LOVE: *life's essential*

There is an old saying, "If you can't love yourself, how the heck can you love somebody else?" This admittedly cheeky statement actually holds a lot of truth but the bottom line is everything starts with self-love—your health, your self-esteem, your relationships, your success, and your happiness. Even if you had a less than ideal childhood, it is never too late to esteem yourself and watch as everything takes a turn for the better, and quickly.

You can weave this strand of personal empowerment into your life and make sure it grows sure and strong. Your body will recognize when you begin regarding it and treating it like a temple instead of just a vehicle to get from point A to point B. Imprint the positive on body and soul with a simple daily ritual that you can incorporate into your morning routine. This involves making a salve you can rub on after your shower or bath. Not only will it refresh your spirit every day but, as a bonus, your skin will actually become smoother and softer than silk.

sanctifying salve: *to heal and restore*

Why pay so much for tiny jars full of chemicals when you can whip up a yummy blend of healing herbs and restorative essential oils yourself? It's far cheaper, healthier, and imbued with your personal magic.

gather together:

1 tablespoon hardened beeswax

5 tablespoons organic oil (sunflower oil is effective and affordable; apricot, jojoba, and avocado oils are nice but quite expensive)

20 drops calendula tincture

10 drops chamomile oil

5 drops lavender oil

½ teaspoon of pure aloe-vera gel

double boiler

whisk and thermometer

small, clean jars with lids

Melt the beeswax with the organic oil in a double boiler (or in a bowl over a saucepan). When the beeswax is fully melted, remove the bowl or pan from the heat. Whisk the mixture until it is cooled to around 100°F (38°C), then stir in the tincture and essential oils along with the aloe vera. Stir gently, thinking of your intended outcome of health, glowing skin, and joy-filled times. The mixture will thicken into a smooth salve but before it stiffens too much, spoon it into the storage jars. Don't forget to label them. Make pretty labels if you are gifting a lucky loved-one this sacred salve. These homemade creams will last longest if you keep them refrigerated.

a calming balm: *make your own*

For those of us who, like me, are not all that crafty, simplicity is key. This basic three-ingredient recipe takes all the fuss and muss away so you even enjoy the process of creating your own calming balm. The concoction will not only soothe and nourish the skin, but also it is very good for your soul.

After experimenting a good bit, I discovered that the fresh and lightly citrus scent of neroli in combination with vanilla is extremely comforting and also tremendously relaxing so I usually add these essential oils. The result is so pleasing, you may even consider using it as a perfume. See opposite for some more essential-oil combinations to try.

gather together:

1 cup (8 oz/225 g) shea butter

½ cup (4 fl oz/125 ml) coconut oil

½ cup (4 fl oz/125 ml) almond oil

15 drops neroli essential oil

15 drops vanilla essential oil

double boiler

wooden spoon and whisk

4-fl oz (125-ml) clean jars with glass lids

Melt the shea butter with the coconut oil in the top of a double boiler. Remove from the heat and allow to cool for 30 minutes. Add in the almond oil (you can substitute olive oil, jojoba oil, or any liquid organic oil) and blend. When the mixture starts to solidify partially, add in 15 drops each of the essential oils. Stir in, and then whip the mixture to a butter-like consistency, which will take a few minutes only. If you're like me and you want to try it immediately, do indulge yourself, you've earned it!

Store the balm in clean, glass-lidded jars in a cool, dry cupboard. This balm also makes a thoughtful gift. A little goes a long way.

More mood-boosting balm blends

Try these combinations for your calm balm and you will soon discover bliss in a bottle:

* **Mellow me:** equal parts of chamomile and rose is a gentle, mellowing combination.

* **In your groove:** bergamot and basil will help you to get your groove back.

* **Chill out:** clary sage and ylang ylang pair up nicely to bring you peace of mind.

* **Unwind your mind:** jasmine and valerian will sweeten up your mood in a jiffy.

* **Happy hippie:** lavender and patchouli are a power duo for a quiet mind and upbeat thinking.

* **Sweet serenity:** lemon balm and vetiver combine for real soothing and letting go.

salts and pepper: *raise-your-spirits ritual*

Earthly elements as simple as salts and pepper can be part of your self-healing. Add the right essential oils into the mix and you have a stimulating and soul-stirring combination. I learned about the strong protective magic of black pepper from the late, great Scott Cunningham himself, pre-eminent authority on all things Wicca. I recommend this as a rite to begin your day in the soft morning light or at twilight, when the sun is weakening. This ritual will both soothe and raise your spirits, offering quiet contentment and a fresh perspective.

gather together:

2 cups (14 oz/400 g) Epsom salts

1 teaspoon black pepper

½ cup (4 fl oz/125 ml) apricot kernel carrier oil (can substitute jojoba)

1 oz (25 g) aloe-vera gel

6 drops sandalwood essential oil

8 drops jasmine essential oil

glass bowl and wooden spoon or paddle

Place the Epsom salts and pepper in the bowl and stir. Now add in the carrier oil and mix well. Lastly, add in the essential oils and stir very well. Shake the mixture together and pour as much as you like into your bath under the running faucet (tap). (The ingredients must be premixed so the power of the oils isn't diluted by the water before their magical properties bond.) This therapeutic soak will do wonders for your mood and your skin. Speak aloud:

My mind is clear,
My spirit soars.
My heart is open,
I am whole,
I am at peace.
And so it is.

As you soak, think of relaxing in your favorite places and reflect upon happy memories of times spent there as you plan new ones. Bask in the steaming water of this healing bath brew.

Divine detox

Your body rids itself of toxins via the lymphatic system. You can speed that process by body brushing, gently stimulating the lymph nodes to do their job even more efficiently. Body brushes look like equestrian grooming tools and are easy to find at any bath and body store, health-food store, or pharmacy. Always use a light touch when dry brushing and, afterward, apply a calm balm, such as "in your groove" or "sweet serenity" (see pages 82–83).

You can double down on wellness by dry brushing before a bath as you are detoxing your skin and body, rehydrating your skin as you are soaking. One third of your body's toxins are excreted through the skin, the largest organ, and dry brushing helps to unclog pores and excretes toxins that get trapped in the skin. A ritual that takes only 5 minutes a day offers so many health benefits, including the lovely bonus of a sense of deep serenity. All you need is a bath tub and a natural bristle brush with a long handle.

Remove your clothes and stand in the empty tub and start bushing at the feet and move upward. Use long upward motions and brush all over your body, using a few brush strokes in every area. When done, rinse the tub thoroughly and rinse yourself. Scandinavians advocate rinsing in cold water too as that stimulates the blood to circulate, bringing more blood to the topmost layers of your skin. I suggest remaining skyclad as you run your ritual bath and perform other ablutions and ceremonial steps, such as lighting candles and mixing oils and salts. Notice how tingly and alive you will feel all over. Self-care is self-healing.

roman chamomile: *a clarity spell*

Roman chamomile essential oil is derived by distilling fresh or dried flowers of this beloved herb. Another frequently used option is German chamomile, which has much smaller flowers. The deep blue German chamomile essential oil is known for its excellent anti-inflammatory properties. When you read about the splendid healing at European spas, they are using one of these two tried-and-true favorites. These treatments have been used for over 2,000 years so that is a good indication of how they have helped. Chamomile oil was used by Roman soldiers to relieve anxiety and to induce a strong sense of purpose as they set out to fight.

In clinical trials, this essential oil has been found to be effective in treating generalized anxiety disorder. A walk in the garden where these delightful little aromatic flowers grow is often considered a sure cure for depression. The sweet scent and the sight of the pure white flowers with sunny yellow centers can raise the spirits.

Similar effects can be obtained by using ¼ cup (2 fl oz/60 ml) of Roman chamomile oil in your bathtub and dabbing a few drops on the pulse points. The vapors can be inhaled or the oil can be used in a diffuser for a generalized effect. Before you step in your Roman chamomile bath, say the following aloud:

Flora, Goddess and giver of flowers,
Today, I need your regenerative powers.
This small sweet herb is here to heal.
With thanks to you, this spell I seal.
Harm to none. So mote it be.

himalayan heightened awareness: *supernatural salt scrub*

This bath soak is marvelous for aromatic relaxation! Lavender, Roman chamomile, neroli, and fresh peppermint go perfectly with magnesium flakes, Epsom salts, and Himalayan pink sea salt. Together they swiftly deliver serenity and a combination of full relaxation and heightened awareness. Magnesium flakes are easily available from health-food stores and pharmacies.

gather together:

handful of fresh mint leaves

½ cup (3½ oz/100 g) Epsom salts

½ cup (3½ oz/100 g) Himalayan pink salt

1 cup (70 oz/200 g) magnesium flakes

1 tablespoon Roman chamomile essential oil

12 drops lavender essential oil

4 drops neroli essential oil

metal bowl

loofah or rough washcloth

While you run a hot bath, crush the mint leaves in your hand and toss them directly into the hot water pouring from the faucet (tap). Now place all the salts in a bowl and gently fold in the magnesium flakes. Lastly, add the essential oils and stir lightly. Now pour half of the mixture under the faucet and when the bath is ready, disrobe and step in. Sit back and enjoy the delightful scent of the fresh mint and aromatherapy salts and oils. After a few minutes, take your loofah or a rough washcloth and use the remaining mix to scrub your skin. Afterward, sit for a spell and enjoy the stimulating sensations. The magnesium actually slows the production of the stress hormone in your body and aids sleep, as well as being marvelous for your skin.

Chapter 6

MEDITATION STATION
Rituals for Relaxation and Letting Go

Our minds are our most powerful tool. It is with directed thought, your intention, that you create enchantment and desired outcomes in your spellwork. By this same token, consciousness management, which is at the core of meditation, is the connecting thread in body, mind, and spirit wellness. I think of meditation as "mental magic" and you can and should harness the power of your brain to deal with stress and difficulty and achieve a higher state of awareness. Many of us start our day with some kind of grounding practice and I begin with an intention-setting meditation.

A calm inner state, which you can cultivate, is instrumental to realizing your deepest goals and intentions. By starting your day grounded and centered, you will experience more balance and flow throughout your day and into each evening. The practice of meditation helps you to raise your energy and self-awareness. By expanding your consciousness, you create a clear, inner space that allows you to move toward the center of your intention. It is from this place of grounded awareness that you can really focus on what's most important to you. Through guided meditations designed to help you relax and center, you'll have an opportunity to hone in and refine your inner vision.

PURIFIED BY FIRE: *incense inspiration*

When we focus on incense sticks during meditation, we move into a mystical space that is both physical and spiritual. Like us, the incense stick is earthbound. It burns for a finite time but the diaphanous spirit it releases is unbound by time or space. Rather than shutting down our senses to focus on an inner realm, incense involves our senses as we follow whirling smoke upward and outward while we take in its scent so that it fills us as we breathe.

The journey starts with a flame, and then a glowing ember releases smoke to rise above us in an ethereal dance. Ashes fall below, purified by the fire. We can use this to imagine negative thoughts being changed from darkness into the beauty of gray snowflakes and a scented spun-silver plume, lighter than air. We can watch as our atmosphere is altered to become reminiscent of the heavens and lifts our thoughts. Embers become shooting stars, and the silver ribbon of smoke becomes unraveled clouds. Altered senses may guide our inspired thoughts to travel along new, perhaps undiscovered, pathways.

We can imagine our physical selves being represented by the incense stick, our inner fire releasing magic into the world. That part of us emanates outward, expanding to mingle with the breath of those around us as we ride the wind to become part of everything.

We can also see in the swirling smoke our life's path, not a straight line but a twirling, meandering ballet that moves us ever onward and upward. We may leave a bit of ourselves behind as we bounce off of our surroundings, working through them, but no matter what we do, we cannot avoid our final destination—oneness with all that is. As spiritual beings enjoying the physical experience of life, incense meditations can help us to remember the beauty and wonder of our existence, where heaven and earth, body and spirit, are all available to us in every moment.

Your handcrafted incense will bring much bliss to your home (see page 92). After lighting it, speak this spell aloud:

Hand and Heart Meditation

Wherever the scent of this incense goes is blessed.
Wherever the smoke of these herbs goes is blessed.
Wherever the fire of these herbs burns is blessed.
By my hands, I made this magic. With my heart, I am grateful.
My home is blessed. My family is blessed. I am blessed.
And so it is.

witch craft: *kitchen cupboard incense*

As you may have noticed, I treasure cinnamon incense. It brings a positive energy to your space with its appealingly sweet and spicy scent. It also brings prosperity and calm. What could be better? This may become one of your favorites, too, and it is truly easy to make.

gather together:

1 tablespoon ground cinnamon

1 teaspoon of water

small bowl

baking sheet

small glass votive container

Spoon the ground cinnamon into the middle of your bowl, add the water, and mix well until the consistency is close to that of damp sand. Use your hands to knead the mixture into your desired shape, which could be a cone, pyramid, ball, or even a heart shape. Place this onto your baking sheet and into the oven at 325°F (160°C/Gas 3) for 15 minutes. Take it out and let it cool to room temperature. Then place it in the glass votive container.

See opposite for more aroma suggestions. These DIY incenses take a few seconds to light but their captivating scents are so worth it.

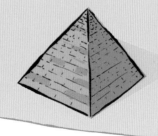

DIY enchanted incenses

Care and storage will help your homemade incense last much longer. I keep mine in a cupboard on a shelf below my candles. There, they are kept dry, and no light comes in. I keep my DIY cones in a double layer of kitchen foil, which can be folded and used as a travel incense burner, too. Lidded cigar-type boxes also offer good options and protect your craft from air and light, which degrade the quality. Small lidded glass jars, like clean baby food jars, are ideal for these baked incense balls and cones. You can also label them with the date, ingredients, and name. Adding a pretty label to a few jars filled with lovingly handmade incense makes a thoughtful and sacred gift. I have kept incenses I made for over a year but since I burn daily, they rarely last that long. When I open my cupboard to unwrap incense, the perfume that wafts out is simply heavenly.

* **Ginger** will bring more money into your space, as well as success.

* **Cardamom** is used in love magic and will also bring you tranquility.

* **Allspice** is quite effective in healing work.

* **Nutmeg** awakens psychic responses and prophetic dreams.

* **Clove** is excellent for invoking protection and banishing negativity.

finding your true north: *guardian moon spell*

This little spell will take you deep inside yourself. It will greatly empower you and instill in you a much deeper understanding of who you are and what you are here to do. Each of us is as individual as a snowflake, and our souls are imprinted with a stamp of specialness. The closer you get to the revelation of your soul's mission, the more you will know why you are here, and more importantly, what you are here to do. That is real magic. The best time to perform this spell is during the dark of the new moon, when the night sky is at its darkest. The new moon is also the best time for initiating the new in your life.

gather together:

compass

athame

1 white votive candle and glass jar

mint essential oil

incense from the list on page 93

paper and pen

Go outside and find a solitary space in which you can use the compass to find true north. When you feel comfortable and safe to begin, cast a circle of energy by pointing your athame in all four directions, starting with north and moving clockwise, or sunwise. Acknowledge each direction as you go and call in the spirit guardians.

Stand in the center of the circle, and with your forefinger, anoint your candle with the essence of mint, a herb that stays strong, green, and alive with healing energy. Place the candle in the glass jar and light it, setting the jar carefully and securely on the ground. Then light the incense with the flame of the candle and put it on the ground beside the candle.

Breathe slowly and deeply. Be mindful that you are here in the darkest night, celebrating the sacred. As you breathe, look around at the majesty of nature and the world around you. Feel the ground beneath your feet. Listen to the silence around you. Now open your heart completely to the awesome power of the universe and the magic both inside and outside of you. With eyes closed, speak aloud:

Standing here beneath the moonless sky,
I open my heart and wonder why
I am here. What is my true north, my turn?
Tonight, I will learn
The reason why I yearn
To serve the Goddess and the God.
This night, I'll hear the reason
I serve this healing moon season.
Guardians, I call on you now!

You may hear an inner voice, or you may hear an outer voice right beside your ear. Listen calmly, staying centered with your two feet on the ground. You will know when it is time for you to leave with your new message and mission. Thank the guardians as you seal the sacred space, being sure to leave everything exactly as you found it. Incense, jar and candle, and matches all leave with you. When you return home, write the message on a slip of paper and place it on your altar, where it will be hidden from any eyes but yours. Place the candle in its jar and any remaining incense on your altar and burn them each dark moon night.

Here's a final thought. You may also want to begin a special journal of your thoughts, inspirations, and actions regarding the message you received. You have now embarked on an exciting new phase of your life's journey. Your journal will help you as you make discovery after discovery. It may evolve into a Book of Shadows, or it may one day become a book like this!

restoring breath: *murcha meditation*

In Sanskrit *murcha* means "to retain," so this is the "retaining breath." *Murcha* will help you to hold on to some of the natural energy that work and life can drain away. This ritual is a yoga exercise for achieving a state of ecstasy through *pranayama*, or yogic breathing, which is the fine art of controlling the flow of oxygen in and out of the lungs. Conscious breathing can vastly improve your health and make you more alert. Done properly, *murcha* will enhance your mental capacity, center you, and create a sense of euphoria.

Sit down on the floor or a mat and make yourself as comfortable as possible. Now close your eyes and calm yourself completely. Begin the process of *murcha* by taking a few mindful breaths. Breathe through your nose. Don't hold your breath; just breathe in and out in a natural manner, but remain aware of your breathing.

When you are ready, take a deeper breath through your nose and visualize the new air and oxygen traveling throughout your body, cleansing and relaxing you. Hold that deeper breath, bend your neck, and bring your chin as close to your lungs and chest as possible. Keep this position for as long as you can do so comfortably. When you need to, raise your head again and slowly exhale through your nose. When your lungs are empty, repeat the *murcha* breath. Repeat this cycle of breathing five times only. After the fifth breath, notice how you feel and be "in the moment." Like most breathing meditations, you will experience a subtle sort of ecstasy with raised energy and a sense of bliss.

In *pranayama*, it is important to remember not to place any stress on your body. Don't hold your breath beyond your comfort level. To do so would be to go against the grain of the technique and teachings of *pranayama*.

With practice, you will notice you can hold your breath naturally and comfortably just a little bit longer each time. As with all things, *pranayama* gets better with practice. The beginning breath cleanses the pulmonary system and raises your energy level.

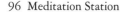

do you know how great you are? *a quiet mind spell*

We live in an age of anxiety. There is so much stress, bad news, and soul-crushing chaos, it is hard to know how to get through each day. But here's the thing—ancient wisdom is the best way to deal with modern troubles. Try the following tried-and-true rite.

gather together:

2 blue candles

palo santo stick and fireproof dish

white paper and blue pen

Any time you feel the need, light the candles and palo santo and speak aloud the following affirmation spell:

Begone from me, worry and woe!
I have the strength to break free and the wisdom to know.
As I breathe this sacred smoke, my calm will grow.
I call upon my inner guide to help me take it slow.
My serenity and tranquility will overflow.
With harm to none, blessings to all.

Repeat this spell three times while the candles and palo santo burn. Inhale deeply ten times and then pass the pen and paper through the sweet-smelling smoke of the palo santo. Now, embrace your intuition and trust it with all your heart. Write down what comes into your mind. You may even feel tingling at the top of your head, which is a very good sign. With your soul's guidance, your inner truth will show you the way through stress-inducing times. Let go of anything that really doesn't matter to you and your loved ones. Read what you have written down and contemplate it. Afterward, extinguish the candles and palo santo. Refer to the paper every day for as long as you need. Use the words of wisdom that came through to you as a guide for your life to sustain you through the stress and strain.

Eco mindfulness walking meditation

Grounding is the technique for centering yourself within your being, getting into your body and out of your head. Grounding is how we reconnect and rebalance ourselves through the power of the element of earth. This is the simplest of rituals, one you can do every day of your life. As you walk, take the time to see what is in your path. For example, my friend Louise takes a bag with her and picks up every piece of garbage in her path. She inspired me to do the same. She does this as an act of love for the earth. During the ten years she has practiced this ritual, she has probably turned a mountain of garbage into recycled glass, paper, and plastic. Louise is very grounded. She is also a happy person who exudes joy and shares it with all in her path.

focal point: *wandering mind rite*

One of the most powerful benefits you gain from having a wand of your own is that it can focus and direct energy, and we all need to do that sometimes! I often experience "monkey mind" when my thoughts race around, and from what I hear from friends and clients this seems to be increasingly common. For that reason, I have been creating more rituals and meditations to counteract a wandering mind, one of the woes of our overbusy world.

First off, you need a wand and they are readily available from new-age shops and also online. Otherwise, if you find a fallen branch that appeals, you can sand it smooth and adorn it to your heart's content by wrapping it with copper wire or other metals and attaching crystals. Have a large one at the end to use as a pointer with which to direct energy and draw circles and other shapes.

The crystal at the end of your wand can also be a marvelous tool for focusing your mind. All you need is a candle corresponding to the color of the crystal. For example, if it is an amethyst, pick a purple candle. Sit in a darkened room, light the candle, and speak this spell while holding your wand and looking through the crystal at the candle flame.

My mind is bright and clear,
I feel no worry or fear.
Into this brilliant crystal I peer.
I call forth focused energy here.
So mote it be.

You may need to repeat the spell, depending on how anxious and worried you are. When you begin to feel quiet and peaceful in mind and body, you can extinguish the candle. Keep it at the ready for when you next need to reel in your wandering mind.

sweeping change: *broom blessing spell*

After I graduated from college, I had one of those experiences we all must endure in our twenties—a bad breakup. I was somewhat of a zombie but my best friend was of a more practical bent. She placed a broom in my hand and suggested I "stop thinking about anything but doing the best possible job sweeping the floor." She was studying Zen Buddhism. I took her advice and even swept the sidewalks once I was done with the small cottage we lived in. Sweeping did bring about a stillness inside me, which was a relief after all the turmoil. I was still hurting but the simplicity of the chores engendered quietude. I have a few brooms, including symbolic besoms, and one is always right outside the back door, ready for the simple ritual of sweeping.

Grab your broom and say aloud as you get started:

No storm outside, no storm within,
With every stroke and every step,
I feel more peace and quiet inside me.
And so it is. Blessed be me.

I have had times when I needed to sweep every floor and even the lawn outside, but it is immensely meditative and I encourage you also to find your Zen.

contentment conjuration: *metta mantras*

When you've had a rough day at work, your inner critic is overactive, or you are just feeling a little down, try this loving-kindness (metta) meditation. It can be difficult to cultivate self-love but it is one of the most important things you can do for yourself. The very peacefulness you create with this ritual you can also send to another.

Begin by sitting quietly, taking relaxed, slow, deep breaths and wishing yourself happiness. After sitting quietly, begin to speak this mantra aloud:

May I be happy.
May I be well.
May I be safe.
May I be peaceful.
May I be at ease.
May I be content.

Continue this practice until you feel full of self-love and compassion. When you are ready to move to the next phase, begin to think of another person to whom you would like to give happiness and unconditional love. Send the love through your meditation and saying these words:

May you be happy.
May you be well.
May you be safe.
May you be peaceful.
May you be at ease.
May you be filled with contentment.

Chapter 7

SOOTHING SIPS
Tonics, Teas, Tisanes, and Blessed Brews

I have always been a tea lover, ever since Auntie Edie taught me how important herbs are as I toddled behind her in her verdant kitchen garden. I was recently reminded of the deep healing of herbal brews, tinctures, and tonics after a bout of flu resulted in a lingering cough that would not go away, even after two trips to the doctor and several prescriptions. This in itself was a cause for worry. What was wrong with me? Nothing worked. In desperation, I studied the notes I'd made in my Book of Shadows on herbal remedies that had achieved good results and decided simply to double my intake of herbal tea. At the end of the first day, the cough was reduced and after a couple of days, no cough! Ever since, I have been evangelizing for drinking herbal brews. They have a power to heal when nothing else will.

We modern witches have a wealth of wisdom on which to draw, handed down to us from the wise women who were general practitioners for their village or tribe. An easy way to incorporate this into your life is to start keeping clean muslin or cheesecloth, big jars, and several colored glass bottles and canning jars with lids for storing your handiwork. We have centuries of recipes for potions and tonics that were used to help and heal the sick, birth babies, bind the wounded, and tend fever and various other maladies. These hedge witches were healers who also helped with melancholy and related issues, which existed before the words stress, anxiety, and depression were ever applied to them. Perhaps Mother Nature is the ultimate wise woman healer as she provides, and has provided, an unlimited supply of natural medicines, which we can employ for mending mind, body, and spirit.

STRAIN SLAYERS AND TENSION TAMERS:
herbs for healing

Mother Nature's wisdom is infinite. The good news is that there are lots of wonderful herbs that are strongly effective against anxiety, and they don't share the same risk of addiction and dependence that comes with pharmaceutical anti-anxiety medications, such as benzodiazepines. Like all medicinals, these herbs and tinctures aren't right for everyone, but they can be tremendously helpful when they're used at the correct dose and are correctly matched to your needs. It's important to remember that herbs aren't like drugs; there's no specific anxiety herb that can be prescribed for you. You are looking for the herb that's the best match for you. Avoid taking any of these herbs (unless otherwise directed by a qualified practitioner) if you're taking prescription medication for sleep, anxiety, or depression.

Tinctures made from natural herbs are gentle and good for you, but I recommend using one at a time for full effect. This way, you will learn something very important—what is most effective for you. Here's what you need to know about some herbs that can help you live more gracefully with anxiety.

Alleviate anxiety with herbs

Remember, these herbs are helpers on your journey to healing your anxiety. All of your other lifestyle practices, including breath work, exercise, journal writing, a healthy diet, and reaching out for support from friends, family, and practitioners, are still important—but there's no question that life with anxiety is a lot easier with safe and effective herbal remedies in your back pocket.

* Kava kava
  This is the most famous anti-anxiety herb, and with good reason. It is more sedating and hypnotic than passionflower and skullcap and has an intriguing taste that almost numbs your mouth. Some people find that it creates a blissed-out feeling. In Polynesia it has a long tradition of use in rituals as well as in medicines for its sedative and pain-relieving properties. You can try using this herb up to three or four times per week to help relieve your anxiety. It's effective as a tea, as a substitute for skullcap in your tincture recipes, or as store-bought capsules, but tea or tincture are best.

* St John's Wort
  This is one of the most relied-upon of all herbal treatments for mild to moderate depression, PMS, perimenopause symptoms, and its general immune- and mood-boosting effects. It is so popular now that you can find the extract at most pharmacies, grocer's, herbal supply stores, and health-food stores. For brighter days, take 300 to 600 milligrams using a dropper under your tongue so it enters your system safely and swiftly. Most places that sell the extract also sell dropper bottles.

* Hibiscus
  Beloved for the heavenly scented perfume of the flowers, hibiscus is also a powerful relaxant and can even lower blood pressure. As if that is not enough, it can help relieve sore throats and colds. As with other herbal applications, steeping a tablespoon of the dried flowers in a cup of freshly boiled water for 10 minutes twice a day produces a healing tea. This sweet-smelling and tasting floral remedy can help you reset and recharge.

simple skullcap tincture: *for comfort and calm*

This simple and easy recipe using the comforting skullcap herb makes a very fine tincture that has many medicinal uses.

gather together:

¼ cup (½ oz/15 g) dried skullcap

2 cups (16 fl oz/450 ml) apple cider vinegar or 1 cup (8 fl oz/225 ml) vodka and 1 cup (8 fl oz/225 ml) water

1-quart (32 fl-oz/1-liter) canning jar

cheesecloth (muslin), a 6-in. (15-cm) square

6-fl oz (175-ml) colored storage jar that seals

label and pen

Put the dried skullcap in the canning jar and carefully pour in the vinegar. Stir well and seal. Place on a dark shelf and shake once a day. After a month, strain through cheesecloth or muslin. Compost the herbal residue in your garden and store the tincture in a colored and sealable glass jar. Lastly, label it and I like to add the astrological information along with phase of the moon.

You may also want to record this in your Book of Shadows—it will be helpful to you and your family to know that tinctures made in the New Taurus Moon, for example, have the most healing power for you, or whichever it turns out to be.

Skullcap herbal helper

Your skullcap tincture will greatly alleviate anxiety and a downward spiral of moods. Even better, it comes in handy as a mouthwash and hair rinse and for ritual baths, and even as a rub for achy joints and sore muscles.

For a cup of skullcap tea, add one teaspoon of the tincture to a cup of hot water, add a teaspoon of honey, stir, and enjoy.

Your tincture will keep for a year but you'll probably use it up much sooner! This kind of kitchen witchery always reminds me of how lucky we are for Mother Nature's bounty. Expressing our gratitude to her adds a sacred aspect to this healing work.

All that we have is thanks to you,
Great goddess, who makes the sky blue.
All that we will receive is thanks to you,
Good goddess, we are grateful for all you do.
This we pray with love eternal and boundless gratitude.

Passionflower relief

Often mistaken for an aphrodisiac because of its seductive name, passionflower is actually the remedy for people who are so burned out and exhausted that all that's left is angst! This is the remedy for people who give and give until they have nothing left for themselves and a head filled with racing thoughts of worry and to-do lists. This plant is effective in both tea and tincture form, but like skullcap, I tend to prefer tinctures for anxiety remedies because they're easy to use and ready in an instant. Try 20 drops of passionflower tincture in a half cup (4 fl oz/125 ml) of water. Ahhhh!

Herbal hygge: healing teas

We might call it kitchen witchery and our Scandinavian friends could say it is how we "get hygge," which means to get as cozy as humanly possible. This newly trendy lifestyle tradition from the frozen north is not just for lazing about, though we greatly appreciate that aspect; it is also a very healthy way of living, including sauna sessions, lots of herbal food and drink, and community spirit, which is an immunity booster on its own. Tea is a mainstay if you want to be healthy and we feel sure wise women and hedge witches in Northern Europe were the first on the hygge bandwagon. So much of our knowledge about herbal teas and tinctures comes from them.

an ambrosial brew

Herbal tea conjures a very powerful alchemy because when you drink it, you take the magic inside.

For an ambrosial brew with the power to calm any storm, add a sliver of ginger root and a pinch each of echinacea and mint to a cup of hot black tea. Before you drink, pray:

This day I pray for calm, for health, for clarity
For me and all others.
I pray for the wisdom to see the beauty
of each waking moment.

Blessing be. Blessings for all.

Tisanes: nurturing with nature

Tisanes are teas that are strictly herbal. Brewing up a tisane is one of the best ways to nourish the soul, ease the mind, and heal the body.

* **Chamomile** is called "sleepy time tea" by some people and they have it right as it makes a wonderful bedtime drink.

* **Raspberry leaf** reduces mood swings, evens glucose levels, and helps to relieve the discomfort of varicose veins.

* **Nettle** raises energy levels, boosts the immune system, and is packed with iron and vitamins.

* **Dandelion root** grounds and centers, provides many minerals and nutrients, and cleanses the liver of toxins.

* **Fennel** awakens and uplifts, freshens the breath, and aids colon health.

* **Peppermint** is a stomach soother that also refreshes mental energy, raises spirits, and promotes serenity.

* **Echinacea** gives an increased and consistent sense of well-being, and prevents colds and flu.

* **Ginger root** calms and cheers, while aiding digestion and circulation and relieving nausea.

Full moon Tea

It amuses me to see how trendy cold brewed coffees and teas have become—hedge witches and wise women have been making these delightful concoctions for centuries. It is the same as making sun tea, which is gently heated by the warmth of the sun but is made at night in the light of the moon. Simply take a quart (liter) canning jar, with a lid, and fill it with cold, pure spring water. Add four herbal teabags of your choice or a large tea ball or muslin bag filled with three heaping tablespoons of dried herbs. Seal the lid on the canning jar and leave it outside or on your windowsill where it will be exposed to the light of the moon. When you awaken in the morning, you will have cold brewed tea. Do make notes in your Book of Shadows for which brews taste best to you. I can tell you that when the full moon is in the signs of Taurus, Cancer, Virgo, Libra, or Pisces, the tea is most delicious to me. My current favorites are ginger-peach and cinnamon-hibiscus. I just made a batch of full moon lunar eclipse tea and it is marvelous.

lavender and chamomile: *Tranquility Tonic*

In the hurly burly of work weeks and packed calendars, we often find ourselves feeling drained and a bit down in the dumps. When we are fatigued, feelings of gloom can arise. At my house we say "a tonic in time saves nine" because this herbal healer can fend off the bad feelings and perk you right up. Herbal tonics, which are concentrated reductions of the herbs, last longer and provide a higher dose of the herb than teas or tisanes.

gather together:

1½ cups (3 oz/80 g) dried lavender

1½ cups (3 oz/80 g) dried chamomile

1 cup (8 fl oz/225 ml) clear alcohol, such as vodka

2 cups (16 fl oz/450 ml) distilled water

clear quart (liter) jar with lid

cheesecloth (muslin), a 6-in. (15-cm) square

dark glass storage jar with lid

Place the dried herbs into your clear jar. Pour in the alcohol. Add in the distilled water, put on the lid securely, and shake for a few minutes until it seems well mixed. Store in a dark cupboard for 30 days, shaking once a day. Then strain through the cheesecloth or muslin into the storage jar and screw the lid on tightly. The lavender and chamomile leavings will make lovely compost for your witch's garden and the liquid tonic will soon prove itself indispensable in your household.

good cheer: *hot toddy healing*

When someone needs cheering up after a long day or is going through hard times, we mix up a quick hot toddy, adding in one of our tonics or tinctures—we keep a constant supply of echinacea and goldenseal tonic for the purpose, using the same recipe as for lavender and chamomile. A hot toddy is traditionally made with hot water, lemon, sugar or honey, and liquor. The herbal tonic adds a higher level of medicinal power, and we also take it at the first sign of a cold or cough.

gather together:

1 tablespoon pure honey

2 teaspoons fresh lemon juice

½ cup (4 fl oz/125 ml) hot water or brewed tea

1 fl oz (30 ml) brandy or bourbon

lemon or ginger slice

10 drops of lavender and chamomile tonic

warm mug

Warm your mug by pouring boiling water into it and letting it sit for 2 minutes. Pour away the hot water and put in the honey and lemon juice. Add hot water or tea and stir until the honey has dissolved. Add the brandy or bourbon, stir, and drop in a lemon slice. A slice of ginger can be substituted for the lemon for extra zing. To finish, add the lavender and chamomile tonic and stir. Nothing is more reassuring than a warm drink served with love.

Blessing for herbal medicine

At the guidance of a master herbalist with whom I apprenticed, I learned to consecrate the remedies I was making, which adds to their efficacy. Herbal healing is a sacred art and invoking the power of nature will strengthen your homemade magic.

Great-hearted goddess of earth so green
We give thanks for your generosity, O Queen.
You give us everything we need to live.
To you, much love and gratitude we give.
Blessed be.

FIND YOUR CELESTIAL ESSENCE: *a floral healer for each sign of the zodiac*

Some of the most blessed of brews are custom designed for us by Mother Nature herself using the wisdom of the sun, moon, and stars. Floral waters and flower essences express emotional benefits differently and each has special healing applications. As we can tell from the mass popularity of Bach's Rescue Remedy, they work wonderfully to abet emotional health, mental outlook, and positivity. The specifics of these curatives can be pretty direct. For example, the flower impatiens helps those who struggle with impatience. Magical, right? I recommend sticking with the recommended dosage of three to four drops taken via the bottle dropper. Below and overleaf you'll find one flower essence for each zodiac sign. Read yours and learn what can work for you.

♈ Aries: impatiens renewal for rams
High-energy Arians race forward, blazing new trails. Patience is not their strong suit. When the going gets tough, rams just hurry on, never stopping, which can be a major source of undue stress and strain. Try impatiens flower essence and you'll discover a wellspring of fortitude.

♉ Taurus: chestnut-bud benefits for bulls
Security-loving Taureans prefer safe harbor and no surprises, but a life of routine can lead to feelings of being stuck in a rut and sameness. Freshen up your day to day with chestnut bud.

♊ **Gemini:** madia mental magic for twins
Curious Geminis are liable to overwork their brains to the point of over-thinking. Preserve your intellectual power with a mental boost. Madia may be a great flower essence to try because it's said to calm the waves of a wandering mind.

♋ **Cancer:** honeysuckle health for crabs
Cancerians have a legendary love of history, so much so that they can start living there. Resist the pull of the past with sweet honeysuckle essence.

♌ **Leo:** borage for brave lions
Loving, giving, and so dramatic, Leos leave nothing behind as they live life at full tilt, which can be emotionally exhausting and lead to many a heartbreak. When this happens, anyone, especially Leos, should turn to borage flower essence. Borage offers encouragement and can move you from sadness and hurt to healing and openheartedness.

♍ **Virgo:** pine helps perfectionists
Sticklers by nature, Virgos work hard to be organized, on time, and have things just so, but none of us is perfect so that can be a setup for failure. Falling short of your own extremely high standards can lead to a swirl of condemnatory self-talk and a cycle of negativity. Reconnect to self-compassion with pine essence.

♎ **Libra:** scleranthus serenity
Librans are often caught in a balancing act of weighing, and reweighing, their options before making a decision, which can lead to vacillation and hesitancy. To spur determination, try scleranthus flower essence, which encourages clear thinking and real balance.

♏ **Scorpio:** holly is holy
Scorpios are the tops for intensity and passions, which can lead to heartache, disappointment, upset, and even anger. Evergreen holly helps you to feel the universe's eternal love and brings balance to your life. If you feel like you are bumping up against endless frustration, tap into holly's holy life-giving energy.

♐ **Sagittarius:** vervain gives vivacity

Energizer bunnies describes Sagittarians. While sharing their ideals with others fuels their *joie de vivre* spirit, such ardent enthusiasm can sometimes lead to setting overly optimistic goals. If you need support in balancing impassioned pursuits with a pragmatic perspective, try vervain flower essence.

♑ **Capricorn:** oak prevents overwhelm

Unbelievably strong, these loveable goats may never stop, which can lead to burnout. Capricorns try to do everything on their own, drawing too much on their own can-do spirit, which can be a grueling path to achieving goals. Oak is a marvelous flower essence for helping to set boundaries, energy preservation, and maintaining rather than draining yourself while you get to the top of that mountain.

♒ **Aquarius:** California wild rose reduces pain and fever; boosts immunity and mood

Water bearers are individuals, forging their own path, and all that freethinking can create distance between themselves and others. Aquarians can become too detached from people, even loved ones, and can also separate from the practicality of their own life. When you feel the gaps growing, turn to California wild rose, which will re-energize your sense of purpose and your ties to the important things in life.

♓ **Pisces:** pink yarrow soothes both jangled nerves and the stomach

Pisceans are deeply empathetic to the point of being psychic and the big issue can be boundaries. Too much taking on of other people's feelings can cause emotional muddles, sadness, depression, anxiety, and overwhelm. Sensitivity and compassion are beautiful as long as you can draw and maintain clear boundaries between yourself and others. Pink yarrow helps you to maintain mental clarity, good self-esteem, and healthy relationships.

Chapter 8

SWEET DREAM CHARMS
Potions, Prayers, and Invocations for a Good Night's Sleep

Several years ago, I went through a phase of waking up at 4 a.m. no matter what time I went to bed. I had just moved after a difficult breakup and was wholly unsettled. My coworkers, who were such kind people that they published the Random Acts of Kindness books, probably noticed as I became more fatigued and bedraggled but said nothing. This went on for many weeks. Finally, I mentioned to my boss that I was having sleep disruptions and she said, "Oh, four a.m.—the hour of anxiety." She had experienced the same. In her case, it was due to hyper-vigilance where she could not "shut down" or stop going over her to-do list in her mind. A brilliant Buddhist, she found that her spiritual practice was her path to restored health and deep rest and then I knew that my path could do the same for me. And it has.

I pondered the wisdom of my Aunt Edie and the hedge witches of yore and realized I had gotten away from my roots. I was a farm girl yet I was spending zero time outdoors. I started going for daily walks in Golden Gate Park, unpacked my witchy tools, oil, and teas, and got some herb pots growing on the windowsills and stoop of my tiny new apartment dwelling. I self-soothed with these simple steps. Not straightaway but soon enough I was sleeping through the night, awakening refreshed.

Sleep itself is healing and these remedies will keep you rested and rosy!

respite rite: *a good night's sleep herbs*

The sweet scent of petals and herbs can bring deep rest when you cast this spell. Try to perform it during a full moon.

gather together:

½ cup (½ oz/15 g) fresh white and pink rose petals

⅓ cup (½ oz/15 g) dried woolly thyme

pinch of ground cinnamon

1 vanilla bean

small lidded box

white paper and pen

white quartz crystal

Mix the flowers and herbs together, and use some to fill the bottom half of the box. Chop the vanilla bean with your bolline and add to the box. Now write down five qualities you wish for in regard to rest and rejuvenation. For example, when I did this a few years ago, I wrote that I wanted to get up an hour earlier each day feeling fresh and ready for the world. Sure enough, I was able to do that after one week. This manifesting magic works! Fold the paper at least once, to fit into the box. Fill up the box with the rest of the flowers and herbs mix. Nestle the crystal in the herbs right at the top, and close the lid. Each night, open the box and take a sniff to remind yourself of your search for true restoration.

an enchanted pillow: *siesta spell*

One way to make sleep easier to come by in your bedroom is to create an enchanted pillow that you can use for deeply restful sleep any time you need it, whether a catnap before dinner and an enjoyable evening after a stressful day, a long night's slumber, or even a workaday pick-me-up. This pillow is very simple to create.

gather together:

2 yards (2 m) of dark blue satin

spool of silver thread and needle

2 lb (1 kg) buckwheat hulls or organic cotton wadding

1 cup (2 oz/50 g) of dried lavender buds

lavender essential oil in a dropper bottle

Cut the fabric into two squares. Lay one square on top of the other with right sides facing. Use your silver thread and needle to sew three sides together. Turn the pillow right side out and stuff it with either the buckwheat hulls or soft cotton wadding, both of which are highly recommended and environmentally safe options. Once you have stuffed your pillow and gotten it to the desired shape, pour in the cup of dried lavender while you say aloud:

Here I rest my head for sleep so sweet.
Here I let go of all cares of the world outside.
Nothing shall keep me from healing rest,
Rapturous respite is my right.
With harm to none.
So mote it be.

Before you sew the last seam to close the pillow, anoint the silver thread with lavender essential oil by lightly touching the bottle dropper to the length of the thread. After you have sewn up the pillow, touch the lavender oil dropper to the silver thread on the other three seams to anoint the pillow fully. Give it a shake to distribute the lavender buds, and now you are ready for nap time.

Sweet dreams: herbal helpers

Hops As we all know, hops are used for beer-making but did you know that, in the form of a tincture, they excel as a sleeping aid and stress-reliever? Women healers claim that hops are very useful to calm hot flashes in menopause. The ideal dosage of 2 to 4 ml before sleep is said to help anxiety.

Catnip Dry a handful of catnip leaves and steep them in boiling water for 5 minutes. Strain as you would any loose tea. Honey helps even more and a cup or two of catnip tea per day will have you in fine fettle, relaxed and ready. This herb is not just for kitties! We humans can benefit from it as a remedy for upset stomachs as well as a way to diminish nervous tension and help with getting rest. Catnip is wonderful for cat naps!

Valerian root Valerian, native to Europe and North America, has long been used to treat anxiety, stress, muscle tension, and insomnia. It contains valerenic acid and valeranon, which help the body relax into a calm state so that sleep can come naturally. You can either chop fresh valerian root with your bolline or use the dried version, which is easily obtained in herb stores. Use the same recipe as for skullcap tincture (see page 106), replacing the skullcap with valerian root, for a dreamy sleep potion that will relax you, body and soul.

soothe your spirit: *massage candles*

Making massage candles is very similar to making any other type of potted candle. I recommend using soy wax because it is soooo gentle on the skin. It also melts easily and stays together in a puddle after melting so it can be reused, good news for us thrifty crafters. If you have an allergy to soy—and it won't irritate your skin unless you do have a soy allergy—you can use beeswax instead. (Nearly every Burt's Bees product uses beeswax.)

Essential oils or cosmetic-grade fragrance oils are added to create a soothing atmosphere (they also prevent beeswax from hardening again and enable your skin to absorb it). All soap-making fragrances that are also soy-candle safe are perfect choices for scenting your massage candles.

Try this recipe to make your first candle. For every 3 oz (75 g) of wax, add 1 fl oz (30 ml) of carrier oil, and ¼ fl oz (8 ml) of fragrance or essential oil. I suggest making two candles in 4-oz (110-g) metal tins while you master this craft.

gather together:

6 oz (175 g) high-quality soy wax

2 fl oz (60 ml) sweet almond carrier oil or vitamin E oil

½ fl oz (15 ml) essential oil

2 x 4-oz (110-g) metal tins

2 x 6-in. (15-cm) candle wicks

double boiler and water

Melt the soy wax with the sweet almond or vitamin E oil in a double boiler over simmering water. Add the essential oil and stir gently to avoid bubbling or spilling. Once the wax has cooled somewhat but is still melted enough to pour, place the wicks in your containers and pour the wax. Allow several hours for the candles to set and harden. Trim the wicks to ¼ in. (5 mm) above the top of the candle, and they're ready to use.

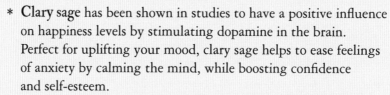

Restful and restorative: essential oils for candle making

Traditionally, these oils are considered to have emotional healing properties and they smell simply marvelous on your skin and in your home. Just burning the candles will be magical!

* **Clary sage** has been shown in studies to have a positive influence on happiness levels by stimulating dopamine in the brain. Perfect for uplifting your mood, clary sage helps to ease feelings of anxiety by calming the mind, while boosting confidence and self-esteem.

* **Cedarwood**, which has a pleasant, woody aroma, acts as a natural sedative. Studies indicate it stimulates serotonin, which, once converted to melatonin, regulates sleep patterns and brings a sense of serenity. A pre-sleep massage with cedarwood essential oil is truly therapeutic and will allow you to rest deeply and awaken refreshed and ready for anything.

* **Lime** smells wonderful, just like the real fruit, fresh and citrusy. It works well to refresh and uplift the mood, and has a lightly invigorating effect, which can work wonders for those suffering from the stress of fatigue, grief, and a sad and heavy heart. Using this essential oil in a massage any time of day will help you to see the bright side of life.

* **Rose** is not just for romance; it is also highly effective for stimulating the mind and promoting a sense of peace, tranquility, and well-being. If you are feeling depressed, worried, or just down in the dumps, rose oil in a massage cream will encourage joy and hope.

* **Jasmine** has been widely noted as among the best for calming the nerves and overcoming stress. For centuries, jasmine oil has been used as a natural remedy for anxiety, melancholy, sleeplessness, and low libido. Jasmine dissipates negativity and helps to stimulate a return to positivity in life.

* **Sandalwood**, which has a lightly sweet and woody scent, aids mental clarity and enhances the ability to focus, and is also supremely grounding. When you're dealing with the challenging demands of a hectic work schedule and long hours, taking time for a massage is essential for your overall well-being and mental health. Sandalwood essential oil offers balance along with promoting feelings of harmony and inner peace.

cross of light: *personal energy shield*

It has happened to all of us. We encounter a person who siphons all energy from us, leaving us drained, fatigued, and emotionally out of sorts. These folks are known as psychic vampires and are usually completely unaware of their unfortunate effect on others. The really bad part is they often leave behind unwanted, negative energy that can be upsetting, and even leave you a bit depressed with odd dreams and sleep disruptions. The good news is there is something you can do about it—create a psychic shield.

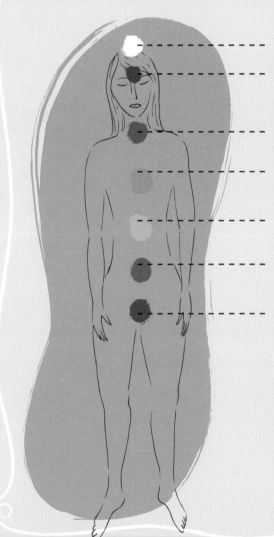

Locating the seven major chakras:

Crown chakra: on the top of the head.

Brow chakra: (also known as the third eye chakra)—in the center of the forehead, above the eyebrows.

Throat chakra: in the center of the throat.

Heart chakra: in the center of the chest.

Solar plexus chakra: behind the soft cartilage at the bottom of the breast bone.

Sacral chakra: just below your belly button. Try placing your thumb on your belly button with your palm on your tummy—your sacral chakra will be under the palm of your hand.

Base chakra: at the coccyx at the base of the spine.

Your **sacral chakra** is associated with the sphere of emotions. It's the center of our feelings and sensations. Opening the sacral chakra will enable you to feel the world around you and also help you understand and manage your own emotional state, central to a sense of balance and well-being.

Use your athame to draw a circle, holding the ritual knife high as you move. Then, to create your cross of light, stand in the circle facing east. Visualize a brightly glowing sphere of white light above your head. Reach inside this ball and pull a beam of light toward you until it touches your eyes. Now speak aloud:

My god and my goddess are above me.

Focus your mind and concentrate on pulling the light beam down through your body, forming a vertical pillar. Touch your second, or sacral, chakra area below your naval and say:

My god and my goddess are below me.

Touch your right shoulder and say:

My god and my goddess are to the right of me.

Draw the light across your body to form a horizontal bar, touch your left shoulder, and say:

My god and my goddess are within me.

Throw your hands and arms upward and outward above your head to form a V and say:

Divine powers within and around me. With Harm to none,
No harm shall come to me. This forms the Cross of Light.

Continue facing east, stretch out your arms to each side, and say:

Before me the power of the earth. Behind me, the power of water.
On my right hand, the power of fire. On my left hand, the power of air.

Now visualize balls of light in each hand that you can wield as a shield. Bow deeply in thanks to the divine powers that provide the light in our lives. If you are traveling on a crowded airplane or attending a busy conference, you might want to perform this rite beforehand to prepare. This is really smart self-care and psychic self-defense. You deserve to keep your own good vibes!

WITCH CRAFT: *DIY enchanted amulets*

Rarely will you see an unjeweled pagan, even if the person is wearing one single ring or pendant. Know full well that jewelry can be used as defense. Witches take it one step further by knowing the meaning, power, and properties of each stone and type of metal, and wielding that energy for the good of others and themselves. The term amulet comes from a Latin word meaning "defense." Indeed, amulets are a way to protect yourself that dates from the earliest human beliefs. Evil eyes might be the most global of all amulets, as they are believed to ward off a hex by simply reflecting it back to its origins. Some amulets were dedicated to a specific god or goddess, offering that deity's sheltering protection.

You can make a powerful protective amulet with just two items— a tiny muslin pouch and a tablespoonful of dried herbs. The list opposite offers a selection from which to choose for the specific kind of safeguard you feel you need. Amulets are very easy to make and make nice gifts, as long as you feel your friend will truly benefit and is aware of the amulet's special qualities and power. If you make one as a small gift to yourself, it will yield big benefits. Wear your amulet as a pendant or tuck it in your pocket or purse for a "guardian to go."

Herbs for amulets

* **Spanish moss** can banish poltergeists and absorb curses, hexes, and black magic.

* **Dandelion** provides shielding energy and also clears away the negative.

* **Marigold** helps you to communicate with the spirit world and those who have passed on.

* **Burdock root** keeps travelers safe and also protects you from anger and jealousy.

* **Clover** will guard against misfortune and invite good faeries into your life.

* **Asphodel** rids your home of unwanted energies and sends a ghost on its way to the afterlife.

* **Betony** keeps sleep disturbances at bay and forestalls nightmares for deep sleep.

* **Agrimony** is a defensive herb used to banish evil spirits and repel hostile magic.

* **High John the conqueror** banishes bad magic and brings good luck to you.

A blessing for protection to say aloud:

I call upon the energies of protection; may all be well,
I call upon the energies of peacefulness; may all be well.
I call upon the energies of positivity; may all be well.
Blessed be me; blessed be thee. All is well under this spell.

prophetic pouch: *dianic dream divination*

This charm will help you to see into your very recent past as well as your near future if you want to understand why you are having sleep disruptions or other issues that are causing upset, sleeplessness, and worry. Often, we might be surprised by what is causing our stress. It is important to figure it out so you can deal with it. Prepare this magical pouch for clairvoyance.

gather together:

lavender, mint, chamomile, and cloves

1 vanilla bean

3 cinnamon sticks

jasmine essential oil

small muslin bag or cloth pouch

Stuff the bag with the herbs. Add the vanilla bean along with the cinnamon sticks, having placed a drop of jasmine oil on both. Tie up the pouch and hold it in both hands until your warmth and energy fully infuse the herbal potpourri mix. Say aloud:

Goddess Diana, Ruler of our Moon,
You are the huntress, brave and true.
Bring me my truth; may I know it soon,
Goddess le Lune; for these blessings from you.
And so it is. Blessed be thee.

Tuck your dream pouch into your pillowcase before bedtime. Have a pen and paper on the nightstand and on waking, record the night's dream. You will receive your answer immediately.

Peaceful potion: divinely restful elixir

An elixir is a very simple potion made by immersing a clean crystal or gemstone in a glass of water for at least 7 hours. Then you remove the stone and drink the water, which carries the vibrational energy of the stone, the very essence of the crystal. This is one of the easiest ways to receive crystal healing and is immediate. Moonstone, tiger's-eye, and turquoise are powerful sleep stones. Leave the crystal in water on your altar or bedroom shrine overnight, if you like, and drink upon awakening. Your life energy will quicken, and you should feel very upbeat and good to go.

SUPERNATURAL SLUMBER: *cord charm*

Cord magic is one of the oldest kinds of enchantment and employs a simple and powerful charm in that it can be used for any purpose in accordance with your intention. After you have set your intention, you tie a knot at each end of the cord, which then acts like a battery, holding the power of your intention as long as the knots at both ends remain intact.

Your magic cord is a rope that binds magic to you. Ideally made from several strands of red wool or ribbon, it should be 9 feet (2.75 meters) long and cut with your bolline. Braid the strands and tie a knot at one end in the form of a loop to represent feminine energy. Leave the opposing end loose or frayed to signify the complementary male energy.

Crystal beads woven into the strands of the rope can compound its magical quality. I recommend that you use clear quartz crystal beads, which are energy amplifiers, but you can use special stones for various effects (see opposite). When you are ready, tie a knot in the loose end.

Stones for your magic cord

 * **Rose quartz** for self-love

 * **Malachite** for protection

 * **Citrine** for grounding

 * **Moonstone** for quiet calm

 * **Jade** for stability

 * **Amethyst** for intuition and psychic ability

 * **Blue lapis** for inspiration

I have an adorned cord in my bedroom on my self-care shrine, which helped to relieve a bout of insomnia some months ago. As I added rose quartz and amethyst beads to the red cord, I held the intention of deep rest, positive dreams, and harmony in my life. I knotted both ends, and since then I have enjoyed exactly that and so can you.

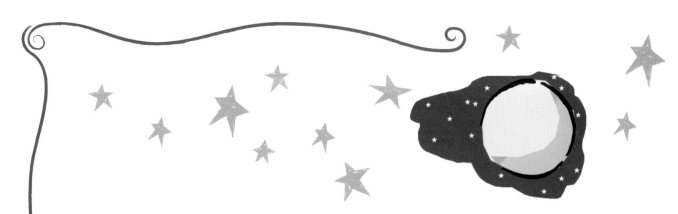

bedtime prayer: *ritual of angel evocation*

We all have matters that weigh us down and keep up
from sleeping. Whether you have an abusive boss, a toxic
relationship, depression, or just feel a little lost, there are
times when you will need the tools to call up guardian energy.
Here is how to get an urgent message out to an angel if you
are in need of protection.

Face the east with your arms by your sides and your head bowed down. Shut your
eyes and with creative visualization envision yourself surrounded by four archangels.
Visualize a pure white light descending from above that expands and surrounds you
and the angels.

Breathe deeply three times and then turn to your right. You are now standing before
the archangel Michael. Open your eyes and say aloud:

Michael, I need your help.

Describe to this highest guardian angel what you need. Give thanks for his aid. Michael
is a true helpmate in time of need. I have done this right before bedtime and woken up
safe, secure, and at peace.

CONCLUSION
Too Blessed To Be Stressed

There is no denying we live in a time of immense tension. So many of us are living under enormous stress and strain but, come to think of it, so were our grandparents and relatives who lived through world wars, the Great Depression, and really hard times. They had far fewer resources than we do now and used simple, homemade methods to deal with anything that came their way. The upside of this "age of anxiety" we are experiencing is that such times can bring people together and strengthen cords of connection, meaning you are closer to your friends, family, and even your spiritual community. At the risk of sounding a bit clichéd, there really are silver linings and this is one. This global stress test has offered an opportunity to practice better self-care, deepen your spirituality, and master many approaches to mind-body management.

For example, you have now learned quite a few meditation practices. Not long ago, the kids and coaches trapped in caves in Thailand revealed that meditation got them through the intense pressure of those most dire circumstances. They overcame the fear, panic, and sense of overwhelm by using their minds and spirit. I sincerely hope none of you encounter anything as severe as that, but you now have an arsenal of tools to help you deal with anything, and practices that will go a long way toward helping you to keep your life in balance. Keep notes in your Book of Shadows or your personal journal about what works for you. You might discover that brewing tonics and tinctures during the new moon in the sign of Taurus and Cancer gives the best result or that essential-oil combinations including bergamot provide calmness for you. My greatest hope for you is this: a home filled with bliss, blessings, comfort, magic, and pure peace of mind!

Your Astrological Guide to Health and Happiness

♈ Aries

March 21–April 19

Ruled by Mars

Cardinal fire sign

Aries is the first of the 12 signs of the zodiac and since it is connected to the element of fire, it's not surprising that Arians receive healing from burning incense, bonfires, and candles.

Soul color: red

Power crystal: sunstone, appropriately red with an incandescent glow, gold-flecked good luck.

Sacred herbs: carnation, cedar, clove, cumin, fennel, juniper, peppermint.

♉ Taurus

April 20–May 20

Ruled by Venus

Fixed earth sign

Taurus is deeply linked to nature and the need for security, a sense of home and place. Taureans can be gifted in the use of wild herbs for healing, growing a kitchen garden and cooking medicinal foods.

Soul color: green

Power crystal: gorgeously marbled green malachite, which is said to help in the regeneration of body cells, create calm and peace, and aid sleep.

Sacred herbs: daisy, lilac, magnolia, oak moss, orchid, plumeria, rose, thyme, vanilla, violet.

♊ Gemini

May 21–June 20

Ruled by Mercury

Air sign

Geminis have keen minds that can sometimes run too fast. Meditation will help to avoid burnout. Singing and chanting are marvelous ways to process all that mental energy and can keep the twins grounded.

Soul color: yellow

Power crystal: moss agate, a great stone for keeping feet on the ground.

Sacred herbs: almond, bergamot, clover, dill, lavender, lily, mint, parsley.

♋ Cancer

June 21–July 22

Ruled by the Moon

Water sign

The moon's phases and signs change as it orbits Earth, and so do Cancerians. They are prone to moods and lunar rituals are truly helpful for these folks.

Soul color: silver

Power crystals: silver and pearls. Cancerians should wear pearls on occasion in honor of their native element of water and to stay secure, refreshed, and relaxed. It will help them to avoid their great nemesis—worry.

Sacred herbs: eucalyptus, gardenia, jasmine, lemon, lotus, rose, myrrh, sandalwood.

♌ Leo

July 23–August 22

Ruled by the Sun

Fire sign

Leos have a lust for life but these brave souls can get worn down. Inspiring and huge of heart, Leos' native creativity can help process inner angst.

Soul color: gold

Power crystal: zircon, believed to be a holy healer that guards against both an excess of pride and resentment.

Sacred herbs: acacia, cinnamon, heliotrope, nutmeg, orange, rosemary.

♍ Virgo

August 23–September 22

Ruled by Mercury

Earth sign

Virgos are both good healers and hypochondriacs. Worry, working too hard, and over-thinking are what these folks need to watch out for.

Soul color: truest blue

Power crystal: labradorite, which reflects every color of the spectrum and can prevent exhaustion. Labradorite encourages Virgos not to become too task-oriented.

Sacred herbs: almond, bergamot, cypress, mace, mint, moss, patchouli.

♎ Libra

September 23–October 22

Ruled by Venus

Air sign

Represented by the scales, Libras seek to create harmony and balance but often the exact opposite happens. When Libras get too out of balance, mood swings and ailments may result. Librans find happiness in love due to their ruling planet.

Soul color: jade green

Power crystal: jade for balance and healthful longevity.

Sacred herbs: catnip, marjoram, spearmint, sweet pea, thyme, vanilla.

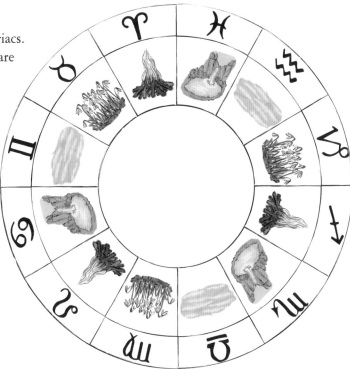

♏ Scorpio

October 23–November 21

Ruled by Pluto

Fixed water sign

Scorpios are intensely passionate and give 1000 percent to everything they do, which can lead to stress, burnout, exhaustion, anger, and emotional wounds. Learning trust and self-love is vital for them.

Soul color: magenta

Power crystal: fluorite. This stone heals bones and wounds that lie beneath the surface, such as broken blood vessels and infections. Secretive Scorpios carry many hurts beneath their strong exteriors, and over time fluorite can gently resolve them.

Sacred herbs: allspice, basil, cumin, galangal, ginger.

♐ Sagittarius

November 22–December 21

Ruled by Jupiter

Fire sign

Sagittarians are forward-thinking, and like to travel and stay on the move. They also have a great capacity for spirituality and philosophy and always seek truth. This can lead to disappointment and avoidance of issues.

Soul color: orange.

Power crystal: turquoise, which is grounding and helps Sagittarians to find their purpose.

Sacred herbs: anise, cedarwood, honeysuckle, sassafras, star anise.

♑ Capricorn

December 22–January 20

Ruled by Saturn

Earth sign

Capricorns are ambitious and will work extremely long hours in an attempt to climb every mountain. This can cause detachment from the heart and damage relationships as well as the body and mind.

Soul color: black

Power crystal: lazulite, opaque and often displaying the dark and cloudy blue associated with the energy of Saturn. Lazulite is good for mental processes and stimulates the frontal lobe.

Sacred herbs: mimosa, vervain, vetiver.

♒ Aquarius

January 21–February 19

Ruled by Uranus

Air sign

Aquarians can be brilliant but very scattered with too many interests and adventures. Dissipation of energies, ignoring health, and focusing entirely on the mind catches up with them and may bring them crashing back to earth.

Soul color: light blue

Power crystal: moldavite, an otherworldly, universal healing, and love stone. Moldavite keeps these very intellectual people in touch with their hearts.

Sacred herbs: almond, citron, cypress, gum acacia, lavender, mimosa, peppermint, pine.

♓ Pisces

February 20–March 20

Ruled by Neptune

Water sign

Pisceans are very receptive, psychic, and sensitive; they can literally feel other people's feelings. This can lead to depression and downward moods unless strong boundaries are created. Self-love and

care of the soul can empower these folks to reach spiritual heights.

Soul color: purple

Power crystal: chrysoprase, perfect for the sign that can attain the highest level of spiritual evolution. Crystal lore says that chrysoprase bridges the awareness of the spiritual and physical self, bringing healing, joy, and laughter. It is said that chrysoprase teaches how to love life and yourself, including your shortcomings.

Sacred herbs: anise, catnip, clove, gardenia, lemon, orris, sarsaparilla, sweet pea.

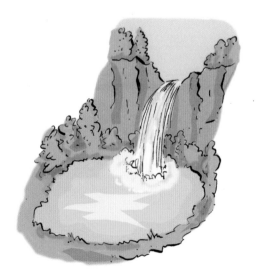

Glossary of Terms

Altar: "raised structure or place used for worship or prayer" upon which a Wiccan practitioner places several symbolic and functional items for the purpose of worshiping the God and Goddess, casting spells, and/or saying chants and prayers.

Athame: *see* magical knives.

Besom: a tool used in Wicca to cleanse and purify a space to be used for ritual; also referred to as a broom.

Bolline: *see* magical knives.

Book of Shadows: a journal in which to keep a record of your magical work. It should also be a book of inspiration for you, filled with your own thoughts, personal poetry, and observations; most helpful if you use it daily or as often as possible.

Candles: represent earth, fire, air, and water. Different colors conjure different enchantments. You can "dress" or anoint the side of the candle with a couple of drops of essential oil using a dropper or cotton ball.

Carrier oil: *see* essential oils.

Cords: knot magic, also called cord magic, involves spellwork using a rope or cord, traditionally red in color. The magic comes from using the physical act of tying and/or untying knots to bind or release the spell.

Essential oils: distillations of herbs and flowers, ideally organic. They retain the fragrance of the original plant from which they are made. When you are making a blend of oils or a potion or lotion, mix them with a carrier (or base) oil, such as jojoba, almond, apricot, grapeseed, or sesame, to dilute the essential oil and make it safe to apply to the skin. Always test a blend on a small area of the skin first and leave for 24 hours to check you don't have any reaction to it.

Incense: powdered herbs, roots, and resins to burn on your altar or in your spells to further your intention. Most New-Age, herb, and health-food stores have a wide variety of cone, stick, and loose incense. Use a sensor or glass dish for burning incense safely.

Magical knives: an athame (pronounced "a-THAW-may") is used to direct the energies raised in your ritual. Since black is the color

Ritual Resources

that absorbs energy, athames should have a dark handle as well as a dull blade, and be placed on the right side of your altar. A bolline is a white-handled knife that is used for making other tools and for cutting materials, such as cords and herbs, in your magical workings.

Palo santo: a tree that grows in South America, similar to cedar and copal (literal meaning is "holy wood"). Burning a palo-santo stick is grounding and clears negative energy, including tension and disquiet. Sticks of palo santo are readily available from New-Age stores.

Smudging: the burning of bundles of sage or other dried herbs to purify and clear a space. Sage bundles are readily available at any New-Age store and are essential to keep on hand for much of your ritual work. You can dry your own herbs for bundling and burning in a fireproof dish.

Wand: rods, ideally made from fallen tree branches, which are used to direct magical workings; instruments used by witches and magicians in spellwork and ritual.

Four major sabbats
Candlemas: February 2
Beltane: May 1
Lammas: August 1
Samhain: October 31

Four lesser sabbats
Vernal equinox: March 20
Summer solstice: June 24
Autumn equinox: September 23
Winter solstice/yule: December 21

Moon phases, sun and moon signs, gardening advice, recipes, how-to instructions for home and garden: almanac.com/topics/astronomy/moon/moon-phase

The Old Farmer's Almanac is also available in print: store.almanac.com/

Lunar lore, herbal lore, astrological information: thewitchesalmanac.com/

Crystals, wands, crystalline statuary, jewelry: crystalage.com/

Runes: guides, supplies, and secrets for reading runes: witchcraftsartisanalchemy.com

Essential oils, carrier oils, soap, and candle-making supplies: junipertreesupplies.com

Incenses, burners, supplies, sages, herbs: herbsandarts.com/incense-burners/

Dried herbs, essential oils, floral waters, books: scarletsage.com/

Study by Dr Robert Emmons, University of California: greatergood.berkeley.edu/images/application_uploads/Emmons-CountingBlessings.pdf

Index

acknowledgments

I consider myself one of the luckiest writers on Earth to be working with Publisher Cindy Richards and CICO Books. No other publishing house expends more effort, artistry, and care on their books. In these days of "spaghetti publishing" when so many presses crank books out on an assembly line, it is quite wonderful to see the craft of bookmaking at its best. The result is stunningly beautiful books that read wonderfully. Michael Hill's illustrations illuminated my ideas and Art Director Sally Powell's hard work is shown in books that are works of art. Designer Eliana Holder's layout is marvelous and copyeditor Marion Paull spun chaff into gold. Carmel Edmonds has been a guiding light for all my CICO books and Dawn Bates was instrumental in making sure this book is the best it can be. Huge thanks to Kristine Pidkameny now a friend for many years and an incredibly wise woman. Thanks to all of you for the honor and privilege of making book magic together.

Bright Blessings!